# PRACTICING THE WRITING PROCESS 2
# THE ESSAY

*BY*
## SHEILA C. CROWELL
*&*
## ELLEN D. KOLBA

**EDUCATIONAL DESIGN, INC.**    **EDI 272**

OCT. 1 7 1995

808.02

ISBN# 0-87694-062-9   EDI 272

# Table of Contents

# Introduction

This book has two purposes:

- First of all, it is an introduction to the writing process. It takes you through the steps that all writers follow, no matter what they write.

- Second, it teaches you to write an essay—a skill that you need both for schoolwork and in order to pass many kinds of tests.

The term **writing process** simply means what people do when they write. Some of these things you may do already. Some may never have been taught to you before. In this book, you will learn what people who write for a living do when they sit down to put words on paper. For instance did you know the following?

- Sometimes you do not know what you really want to write about until you start writing.

- Thinking is part of writing.

- Putting words down on paper—any words—can help get your ideas flowing.

- It is all right to change your mind while you are writing—and to change what you have written.

- There are all kinds of special tricks you can use to make the job of writing easier.

This book will take you step by step through the process of writing the way a real writer does.

- It will help you get started.

- It will show you how to turn your ideas into sentences and paragaphs.

- It will give you practice in improving what you have written.

- If you have a computer with a word-processing program, it will help you make the most of it.

As it helps you discover what the writing process is, this book will also guide you through the process of writing an essay.

Most of your time will be spent on the kind of essay known as a **personal** essay. In a personal essay, you describe how you feel about someone or something that you know about. (This kind of essay is also sometimes called an **expressive** essay because it shows, or expresses, how you feel. A third way of describing the personal essay is the term **narrative-descriptive**. This name tells how a personal essay is written: It often combines sections of description with a narrative, or story.)

You will learn to write a personal essay by observing another student go through the process and then by practicing on your own. At the end of this book, you will apply what you have learned about the writing process and about the writing of an essay to two other kinds of essays: the **expository** essay and the **persuasive** essay. You will also learn some ways to condense the steps in the writing process so that writing a **timed essay** is easier.

Most of all, what you will be doing throughout this book is learning a method—a way of thinking and of expressing yourself—that you will be able to use no matter what you write.

# *PREWRITING*

If you look at the Table of Contents, you will see that there are more lessons in Prewriting than there are in Writing, Revising, or Editing. That alone should tell you how important prewriting is.

Prewriting is the step that starts you on your way to writing. Without it, you couldn't even begin. It helps you with all of the following:

- Getting an idea on your own.

- Writing about a topic that has been assigned to you.

- Deciding who your audience is.

- Setting a purpose.

- Finding out what you really want to say.

- Organizing your ideas.

- Arranging your ideas in the most convincing way.

Best of all, when you finish prewriting, you will have some of the writing done, without even worrying about it.

This section will start you on writing a personal essay from an assigned topic. Each lesson except the first begins with a warmup that gives you practice with some of the techniques used by professional writers. Then you will see how another student uses those techniques to work on an essay. Finally, you will begin writing your own essay.

# Getting Ideas

*Knowing how to choose a topic is the first step in writing well.*

What happens inside your head when your teacher gives you either one of these assignments?

For Friday, write a short essay. You choose the topic.

Write three good paragraphs about the most interesting thing that has happened in your life so far.

Does the inside of your head look like this?

A blank

ZERO

ABSOLUTELY NOTHING

When your mind is a blank, you need a way to get started. You need something that will help you unlock those doors in your brain that clanged shut as soon as you were asked to write. The something that you will use is called **brainstorming**.

Brainstorming is a technique used by artists, business people, inventors, writers, scientists—in other words, by just about everybody who needs to get ideas out fast. Here's how it works.

When writers at an advertising agency have to come up with a name for something—say, a new line of sports clothes—they hold a brainstorming session. The rules are simple:

1. You can say anything that comes to mind—NO MATTER WHAT IT IS.
2. No one criticizes or even comments on what anyone else has said—NOT EVEN IF THEY THINK IT'S WRONG.

Someone in the meeting usually acts as a recorder to write all the ideas on a chart that everyone can see. All the ideas are written down. At the end of the session—which usually lasts about an hour—the group will usually find one or more names that they really like.

Brainstorming works because you don't stop the flow of ideas. If someone says, "No, I don't like that," everyone in the room feels the mental gates begin to close. By letting all the ideas come out without criticism, the group gets a chance to see and choose among as many ideas as they have time to listen to. This kind of brainstorming has proved very effective; however, you cannot always use it in the classroom. When you are taking a writing exam or working at home on a paper, you will need to learn three other techniques that start the ideas flowing. **Free-writing** is a good way of finding a topic or the focus of a topic; once you have chosen a topic, **list-making**, **asking questions**, and **clustering** will help you find out what you want to say about the topic.

1. *Free-writing* helps you get started by making you put words—any words—directly on your paper. It's like brainstorming on paper. You write everything you can think of, about any subject that comes to your mind. You don't stop writing even if you can't think of anything to say. Eventually, the thoughts that lie below the surface—in your unconscious mind—will come out on paper. Here's an example of Tom's free-writing.

*nothing to say     nothing to write about     why do they always do this? I hate*

*writing essays every week especially when school starts     why do they always*

*make us write     why does school start in September     it's too good a month to*

*be inside     it's still light out     the water's still warm enough for swimming*

*but my summer job is over     that was the best job     I ever had     and it paid*

*the most money the most I ever earned     I guess I'll put some of it away . . .*

Tom found two topics in the course of free-writing. The first topic could become an essay titled "Why Does School Start in September?" and the second topic could become "The Best Summer Job I Ever Had."

When you free-write, you don't have to worry about punctuation or spelling. Just write all your thoughts as they come to you, but leave extra space between each group of thoughts so that they will be easier to read.

**Try It 1**

Your assignment is to find something to write about. Begin free-writing and continue until you have filled all the lines.

_____

_____

_____

_____

_____

_____

_____

2. **List-making** can help you find out what you want to say about a topic and can show how ideas are related to each other. Here is a list that Tom made about his summer job.

> *best summer job*
>
>> *always wanted to work at the beach*
>>
>> *easy to get to*
>>
>> *outdoor job*
>>
>> *good boss*
>>
>> *learned some new things*
>>
>> *good pay*
>
> *not like other jobs*
>
>> *first job—underpaid and overworked*
>>
>> *babysitting—too boring*
>>
>> *mowing lawns—no one to talk to*
>
> *next summer job*
>
>> *same as this year?*
>>
>> *get job at clam hut*
>>
>> *cooking is fun*

When he had finished his list, he realized that his thoughts fell into three groups, each of which could become a paragraph. He circled the three phrases that headed each group. He would write about why he liked this job, why he didn't like other jobs, and what he wanted to do next summer.

---

**Try It 2**

Choose a topic from your free-writing sample and make a list. How many groups of ideas do you have?

_____

_____

_____

_____

_____

_____

_____

_____

_____

---

3. **Asking questions** is a technique that newspaper reporters use when they start to shape a story. They ask the following questions because they know that their readers want to know the answers.

> **Who** did it?
> **What** happened?
> **When** did it happen?
> **Where** did it happen?
> **Why** did it happen?
> **How** did it happen?

If you are writing an article for a newspaper, these are good questions to start with. When you write a personal essay, you will choose other questions that someone reading your paper would like to see answered. Here is Tom's list of questions on the topic of the summer job.

> *What was the job?*
> *Why did I like it?*
> *How was it different from other jobs I've had?*
> *Did I learn anything new?*
> *Do I want to go back there?*
> *What kind of jobs do I like?*
> *What kind don't I like and why?*
> *Is pay or people more important to me?*

---

**Try It 3**

On a separate piece of paper, write some questions about one of the topics that came to mind in your free-writing. Use a list to write some answers to your questions.

_____

_____

_____

_____

_____

_____

_____

_____

---

4. **Clustering**—sometimes called **mind-mapping**—is a kind of doodling that combines words, circles, and lines. It is another way of showing all the ideas you have about a topic and how they are related. Here is how Tom uses clustering to arrange some of his thoughts about summer jobs.

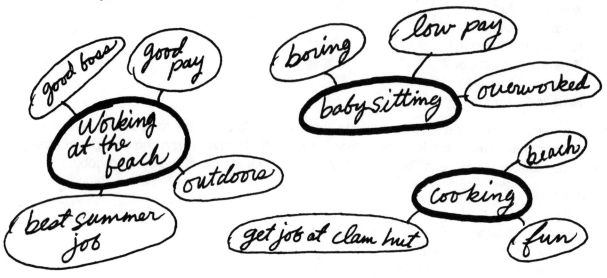

**Try It 4**

Use the clustering technique in the space below to develop one of the topics you thought of in free-writing.

# *Working from an Assigned Topic*

*You write well when you can find something in a topic that you care about.*

## WARMUP

Sometimes you seem to have no choice about what to write. The topic is assigned to you. It might be something interesting. It also might be something you have written about a dozen times before—"My Ideal Vacation," "The Person I Most Admire," "The Book That Has Influenced Me the Most"—and you did not care about it any of those times, either. Much school writing is done on topics like these, and much of it ends up being dull. It is difficult to write well about something that does not interest you.

### Try It 1

Here is a list of essay topics. Some of them will seem interesting and exciting to you. Others will seem boring or uninspiring. Put a plus sign (+) next to each topic that you think you would enjoy writing about. Put a zero (0) next to each topic that you would have to work at in order to find something to write about. (There are no right or wrong answers; everyone will react differently to these topics.)

1. Do you believe the old saying, "Nothing ever stays the same"? Tell about something in your life that illustrates why or why not you think this saying is true.
2. Can secrets be dangerous? Tell about an incident that shows why or why not.
3. Is there someone you would like to get to know better? Describe him or her and explain why you would like to be better acquainted.
4. Think of an adult you know well. What do you think this person was like as a young child? What makes you think so?
5. Think of a book that has influenced you a great deal. Describe the book and tell why it has been so important to you.
6. Think of someone you like now but did not when you first met. Describe the person and explain why your feelings changed.
7. Think of someone you do not like now but did when you first met. Describe the person and explain why your feelings changed.
8. Is it a good thing to expect a great deal out of life, or does that attitude lead to disappointment? Illustrate your point of view by telling about your own experience.
9. If you could spend a vacation any way you liked, what would you do? Why?
10. Would you describe yourself as an adult yet? Why or why not?
11. What is the most frightening thing that has ever happened to you? Why was it so frightening?
12. Who is the person you most admire? It can be someone living or dead, famous or unknown. Describe the person and tell why you admire him or her.

What can you do when you <u>must</u> write on an assigned topic? The topic may seem too broad, or it may seem uninteresting to you, or you may just find yourself unable to think of anything to say on that subject. You might be tempted to write about something else altogether. If it is something you feel strongly about, you would probably write a much better essay than if you wrote about something you did not care about. Unfortunately, though, your grade would probably suffer because you did not stick to the topic.

There is another solution. ***No matter what topic is assigned, there is usually some way to turn it into your own topic.*** For instance, Gloria really hates cold weather. She might begin an essay on an ideal vacation something like this:

Because I hate cold weather, my ideal vacation would take place on

a tropical beach where the temperature is always warm and

it never rains.

Suppose this does not express the way her friend Christine feels about vacations, though. Can Christine approach the topic from another direction? For example, Christine might secretly believe that vacations are always disappointing—that they are never as good as people expect them to be. She might want to start the essay like this:

The best vacation I can imagine is one in which I do not start off ex-

pecting anything special to happen.

No matter what topic has been assigned, you can find something in it that interests you and makes you want to write. All you need are some brainstorming techniques—like the ones you used to find a topic in the first lesson—to help you discover the hidden ideas.

---

**Try It 2**

One way of getting new ideas is to let your mind make connections, or associations, with the topics that have been given to you. To practice this, look at the word at the beginning of each column below. Then beneath it, write as many different words as the word given to you suggests. Do not stop to think. Just write whatever comes into your mind. When you have finished, review the list. Do any of the associations surprise you? Do any give you new ideas?

**gravel**

_____          _____

_____          _____

_____          _____

_____          _____

_____          _____

**chilly**

continued...

**collapse**

_____

_____

_____

_____

_____

**puff**

_____

_____

_____

_____

_____

**Try It 3**

Here is another way of getting ideas. Look again at the topics you worked with on page 13. Choose three of the topics you marked with a zero. Write them below. Then in the space following each one, write at least four ideas (more if you can) that you could turn into an essay on that topic. Remember that this is a brainstorming exercise. You should not try to edit your ideas mentally. Just put them down as they occur to you.

1.  TOPIC: _____

    IDEAS: _____

    _____

    _____

    _____

2.  TOPIC: _____

    IDEAS: _____

    _____

    _____

    _____

3.  TOPIC: _____

    IDEAS: _____

    _____

    _____

    _____

Look at the ideas you wrote under each topic. Which one in each group do you think you can write about? Circle that idea.

# PRACTICING THE PROCESS

## Gerry's Essay

Gerry's class has been assigned the following topic:

> If you could look into the future, what would you see? Describe a typical day in the year 2000, and tell how you will feel about the changes that you see ahead.

Each student must write an essay that is three to five paragraphs long, interesting, and well organized. Gerry is sure that he could handle this assignment if only he could think of what to say. His mind is a blank—until he remembers the brainstorming activities and decides to use them. Here is the list of ideas Gerry writes, with the ones that interest him the most circled.

| | |
|---|---|
| where people live | what buildings look like |
| what cars are like | jobs |
| computers | telephones |
| sports | shopping |
| movies | T.V. |
| kinds of buses, trains | food—how it's cooked |
|    planes | what people eat |
| space travel | clothes |
| money—banks | newspapers |
| books | school |
| pets | robots that work for you |
| music—synthesizers | |

---

**Your Essay** [WP] This symbol is for Word Processor users. If you have a Word Processor, use it for this activity and save the file.

You are going to be asked to write an essay on the following topic:

> If you could live in any period of time—past, present, or future—which would you choose and why? Write an essay describing your choice and the reasons for your choice.

Like Gerry, you will have to write three to five paragraphs that are interesting and well organized. And like Gerry, you may feel right now that you do not have the vaguest idea of what to say. Your first step, then, will be to brainstorm ideas. Even if you already know what you want to write about, try brainstorming first. You may discover a new and helpful direction for your essay. When you have written as many ideas as you can think of, read them over and circle the ones you want most to write about.

_____

_____

_____

_____

_____

_____

# *Deciding Who Your Audience Is*

## *You write well when you know for whom you are writing.*

### WARMUP

Have you ever answered the phone, sure that it was a friend calling, and said something like, "City Nut House, Head Keeper speaking"? If you were lucky and it was a good friend on the other end of the line, he or she probably laughed and made a joke in response. If you were unlucky, it was a stranger, and you ended up being embarrassed.

It is very important to know who your audience is before you open your mouth, or uncap your pen, or sit down at your typewriter or your word processor. You need to know who will be reading what you write, not just to avoid embarrassment but in order to know what to say and how to say it.

Sometimes it is easy to know who your audience is. When you write a letter, for instance, the audience is clearly identified for you—the editor of the school paper, or your Aunt Betsy, or your best friend, who has just moved away. What you want to say is also clearly defined—you disagree with the opinion expressed in last week's editorial, or you are thrilled with the beautiful scarf you received for your birthday, or you have the most interesting news about what really happened at half time during last week's basketball game.

---

**Try It 1**

Read the letter below. As you read, try to figure out who William is and who the letter might be from.

*May 17, 1989*

*My dear William,*

*The birthday gift you sent arrived right on time and was a great surprise. Did you choose it all by yourself? Thank you for remembering how much I like fresh flowers. The yellow lilies in your bouquet remind me of the ones we found in the woods last summer. Do you remember them? This year when you come to visit, you will be big enough to help me plant some lilies in the garden. What colors do you think we should have?*

*Write to me soon and tell me how you like school. Also, send me a new picture of yourself to put on my piano.*

*Fondly,*

continued . . .

Now, answer the following questions. Use the answers to help you decide who the audience is for this letter.

1. Who wrote the letter? What is his or her relationship to William, the person receiving the letter?

   _____

2. How old is William?

   _____

3. What do William and the letter-writer have in common?

   _____

4. How is William different from the letter-writer?

   _____

5. How does the person writing the letter feel about William?

   _____

Whenever you write, you need to have a clear picture of whom you are writing for and why you are writing. You need to keep in mind what your audience is like personally, what your relationship to your audience is, how much your audience knows, and what opinions or expectations your audience has.

**Try It 2**

For each of these assignments, write five questions about your audience that will help you decide what to say and how to say it. Your questions should be very specific. The first one in each group is given as an example.

**A.** A letter to someone you have never met but who knows your best friend. This person has seen your picture, thinks you look interesting, and wants to get to know you better.

1. *How old is he or she?* _____

2. _____

3. _____

4. _____

5. _____

continued . . .

**B.** A newspaper article about the compaint that there is no "school spirit" in your school.

1. *How many of the readers will be students at my school?*

2. _____

3. _____

4. _____

5. _____

**C.** A review of a new science fiction sitcom on television.

1. *Have the readers seen this show yet?*

2. _____

3. _____

4. _____

5. _____

## PRACTICING THE PROCESS

### Gerry's Essay

Gerry is having trouble focusing his essay. Even though he has narrowed his topic, there are still many ways of approaching it. Thinking over all the possibilities, Gerry realizes what his problem is. He does not have a clear idea of who his audience is. Since the essay is a school assignment, he knows he is talking to his teacher, not his friends or the general public. He knows, too, that he will write a better essay if he assumes that his teacher really wants to know what he thinks. As a result, Gerry has some questions about the essay and its audience. Is his audience—the teacher—someone who wants to help him plan his future, someone who wants to know more about what he is like, or just someone who wants to be entertained by a good story?

Gerry draws up the following list and checks each item that he thinks describes his audience.

My reader wants to know what special knowledge I have about the subject.
My reader wants to know how well I understand the subject.
↘ My reader wants to know whether I have any special ideas or insights about the subject.
My reader wants to know how much I like the subject.
↘ My reader wants to know more about me personally.
My reader wants to be entertained by me.
My reader wants to be convinced that my point of view is right.
↘ My reader wants to know how well I can write.

## Your Essay WP

Your essay is also a school assignment, and your audience is your teacher. Like Gerry, though, you still have some things to decide about your audience. Here is the list Gerry used. Read it and check each item that you think describes your audience.

My reader wants to know what special knowledge I have about the subject.

My reader wants to know how well I understand the subject.

My reader wants to know whether I have any special ideas or insights about the subject.

My reader wants to know how much I like the subject.

My reader wants to know more about me personally.

My reader wants to be entertained by me.

My reader wants to be convinced that my point of view is right.

My reader wants to know how well I can write.

# Making Sure Your Subject Is Complete

*The subject you choose must fit the assignment.*

## WARMUP

Your topic has been assigned, and you have chosen something to write about for that topic. You are not ready to start writing, though, until you are completely sure that the subject you have chosen fits the assignment. The first step is to make sure that you have read the assigned topic correctly and understand what it includes.

---

**Try It 1**

Here is the list of essay topics from Lesson 2. Because these are all topics for a personal essay that will combine narration and description, they are structured in a special way. The topic usually begins with a question or a statement. Then it asks you to describe someone or something or to tell about something that has happened to you. Finally, it asks you to tell why you think or feel as you do.

Underneath each topic below, write in your own words the two things it asks you to tell about. The first one is done for you as an example.

1. Do you believe the old saying, "Nothing ever stays the same"? Tell about something in your life that illustrates why or why not you think this saying is true.

   *Describe something in your life. Show why or why not you think the*

   *saying is true.*

2. Can secrets be dangerous? Tell about an incident that shows why or why not.

   _____

   _____

3. Is there someone you would like to get to know better? Describe him or her and explain why you would like to be better acquainted.

   _____

   _____

4. Think of an adult you know well. What do you think this person was like as a young child? What makes you think so?

   _____

   _____

continued . . .

5. Think of a book that has influenced you a great deal. Describe the book and tell why it has been so important to you.

   _____

   _____

6. Think of someone you like now but did not when you first met. Describe the person and explain why your feelings changed.

   _____

   _____

7. Think of someone you do not like now but did when you first met. Describe the person and explain why your feelings changed.

   _____

   _____

8. Is it a good thing to expect a great deal out of life, or does that attitude lead to disappointment? Illustrate your point of view by telling about your own experience.

   _____

   _____

9. If you could spend a vacation any way you liked, what would you do? Why?

   _____

   _____

10. Would you describe yourself as an adult yet? Why or why not?

   _____

   _____

11. What is the most frightening thing that has ever happened to you? Why was it so frightening?

   _____

   _____

12. Who is the person you most admire? It can be someone living or dead, famous or unknown. Describe the person and tell why you admire him or her.

   _____

   _____

The second step in making sure your topic fits the assignment is to make sure that you will be able to write three to five paragraphs about the subject you have chosen. An easy way to check is to write at least three subtopics for the subject and then see whether they cover the topic completely. For instance, if Topic 4 were assigned to you and you chose to write about what your Uncle Albert was like as a child, you might generate these three subtopics:

1. Probably drove his parents and teachers crazy because as an adult he still likes to do wild and unexpected things.
2. Probably was popular with other kids because as an adult he has lots of friends.
3. Probably never sat still because as an adult he always has dozens of projects going at once.

You can see that each subtopic gives a specific detail about Uncle Albert as a child and a reason for choosing that detail. Both parts of the topic are covered, and there is enough material for at least three paragraphs.

Suppose, however, that you choose these three subtopics instead:

1. Probably drove his parents and teachers crazy.
2. Probably was popular with other kids.
3. Probably never sat still.

You still have enough material for three paragraphs, but you have covered only one part of the assignment—what you imagine Uncle Albert was like as a child. You have not covered the other part of the assignment—to tell <u>why</u> you think so. Your topic outline is not complete. If you cannot think of the details you need in order to cover the topic fully, you may need to think about choosing a different subject.

---

**Try It 2**

Here are some of the assigned topics with possible personal subjects. Several subtopics have been written under each personal subject. In each case, decide whether the subtopics cover the assigned topic completely and whether they could be developed into a three- to five-paragraph essay. If you think the essay can be developed fully from these subtopics, put a plus sign (+) in the blank. If you think it cannot be developed fully, put a zero (0) in the blank.

_____ 1. Think of someone you like now but did not when you first met. Describe the person and explain why your feelings changed. *[Eddy Winter]*
  a. Seemed like a stuck-up snob at first but is friendly now.
  b. Got to know him when we worked on a science project together.
  c. Found out that he's really afraid other people won't like him.

_____ 2. Think of someone you do not like now but did when you first met. Describe the person and explain why your feelings changed. *[Dorothy Peterson]*
  a. Seemed pretty nice at first and we talked on the phone a lot.
  b. Used to be one of my best friends and ate lunch with me every day.
  c. Is the smartest person in our math class but isn't so great in English.

continued...

_____ 3. If you could spend a vacation any way you liked, what would you do? Why? *[Go to a big resort hotel]*
a. Swim and play tennis every day and take lessons with the tennis pro.
b. Buy new clothes for my vacation and borrow my brother's Walkman.
c. Go to the disco every night and meet tons of new people.

_____ 4. What is the most frightening thing that ever happened to you? Why was it so frightening? *[Getting lost on a mountain trail]*
a. Got separated from rest of group and couldn't find right trail.
b. Had never been hiking before, so didn't know what to do.
c. It was getting dark, and I didn't have a flashlight.

## PRACTICING THE PROCESS

### Gerry's Essay

Gerry is ready to make sure that he has understood the topic assigned to his class and that what he has chosen to write about fits that topic. First he rereads the topic and writes the two things he will have to tell about.

If you could look into the future, what would you see? Describe a typical day in the year 2000 and tell how you feel about the changes you see ahead.

*1. Tell what a day in the year 2000 will be like.*

*2. Say how I feel about these changes.*

Then Gerry writes three subtopics that use the ideas he has chosen from his brainstorming list:

*a. Where I will live and what my life at home will be like.*
*b. What life at work and after work will be like.*
*c. How I will feel.*

He reads over these subtopics and decides that the third one—how I will feel—is too general. He crosses it out and changes it to

*c. How technology has made some things better and some things worse.*

---

**Your Essay** WP

Read the assigned topic again.

If you could live in any period of time—past, present, or future—which would you choose and why? Write an essay describing your choice and the reasons for your choice.

Now write the two things this topic asks you to tell about.

1. _____

2. _____

continued...

In the blank below, write the subject you chose for this topic in Lesson 2.

_____

Then write three subtopics for this subject. The subtopics should cover the assigned topic completely. They should also show that you will have enough material for three to five paragraphs.

a. _____

   _____

b. _____

   _____

c. _____

   _____

# Turning Your Ideas into a Statement

*Writing one sentence that tells what your essay is about gives direction to your writing.*

## WARMUP

The words you choose when you write about a topic helps set the tone of your essay. It is the tone that lets your reader know how you feel about your subject. The tone can be personal or objective. It can be serious or humorous.

A sentence or a paragraph that has a **personal** tone usually contains the personal pronouns *I*, *me*, *my*, *you*, *your*. Contractions like *it's* and *don't* are often used. In **objective** writing, contractions are not used. Neither are personal pronouns, since the writer must stand aside from the topic and look at it as if it were an object to be studied.

**Serious** writing is the kind of writing that most people do most of the time. It looks at the topic directly and says to the reader, "Listen to me. I really mean this." **Humorous** writing, on the other hand, tries to look at something from a totally unexpected angle. It says to the reader, "Can you believe this—especially the way I'm showing it to you?"

| | |
|---|---|
| **SERIOUS PERSONAL** | Writing essays about myself has never been an easy thing for me to do. It's not that I don't think about myself a lot. I probably think about myself more than most people I know. It's just that I don't always like what I see. |
| **SERIOUS OBJECTIVE** | Does the right to vote at eighteen mean that all eighteen-year-olds are mature? The answer to that question depends on how the word "mature" is defined. According to *Webster's Collegiate Dictionary*, something can be called mature if it has completed its development. |

A humorous sentence or paragraph can be either personal or objective. The humor often comes from looking at two very unlike things as if they were very much alike—dogs and cats for example. Humor is also the result of exaggeration—the writer compares teenagers to wild animals.

| | |
|---|---|
| **HUMOROUS PERSONAL** | We should have realized that life with Darth would always be exciting when she was kicked out of Puppy Obedience School. She's big and playful and good-tempered—most of the time—but she never listens and she can never be made to feel guilty. In fact, she acts like a cat in a very large dog costume. |
| **HUMOROUS OBJECTIVE** | When dogs first came to live with humans, some people were very worried about how they could control these large beasts with very sharp teeth. After all, for thousands of years humans and wolves had been enemies and had damaged each other quite a lot. Then a wise cave parent looked around at the large cave teenagers and said, "It's easy to control something stronger than yourself. Make it feel guilty." |

**Try It**

Imagine that you are writing an essay on after-school activities. This is what you have on your topic so far.

> *clubs, sports, studies*
>> *getting in with the group you like*
>> *conflicts with after-school job*
>> *problems in keeping up grades*
>> *clubs look good on job and college applications*

You're not sure what tone you want to take, so you turn some of your ideas into sentences:

1. Choosing the right after-school activities is as important as choosing the right courses. After all, learning is not just something that takes place in a classroom.

2. My guidance counselor was a little surprised when I told her I'd have to drop chemistry because it conflicted with Drama Club. She practically fell off her chair when I told her that history was out too because I needed the time for extra basketball practice.

3. At the beginning of this year, I was faced with a big decision—cut down on after-school activities or cut out my after-school job. On the one hand, I needed to start saving for college. On the other hand, the clubs I belonged to showed I was a well-rounded student.

4. If after-school activities were held in the morning, principals would be amazed at how few students were late to class. Cheerleaders would be jumping and cheering twenty minutes before the first bell; the drama club would hold its first rehearsal at seven— and everyone would show up.

Write the number of the sentence that best answers the following questions.

1. Which opening sentence shows a SERIOUS, PERSONAL TONE? _____

2. Which opening sentence shows a HUMOROUS, PERSONAL TONE? _____

3. Which opening sentence shows a SERIOUS, OBJECTIVE TONE? _____

4. Which opening sentence shows a HUMOROUS, OBJECTIVE TONE? _____

## PRACTICING THE PROCESS

### Gerry's Essay

Gerry looks at the notes he has made about his topic.

> a. *How technology will make my life different*
> b. *Details of my day—beginning to end*
> c. *What I will like, what I won't like, and why*

He has already decided on his audience—his teacher—but he doesn't know what tone he should take. One way to find the right tone is to decide what the purpose of his essay is. This is what he writes.

PURPOSE  *My essay will be about a typical day in my life in the year 2000 and it will include lots of details about technological changes at home and on the job. It will also tell how I feel about those changes.*

By writing the purpose—which is in addition a short description of his essay—Gerry realizes that he has also identified the tone his essay should have. Because he wants to describe a lot of factual things very accurately, a serious tone is appropriate. Since he also wants to show how he feels about these changes, he will use the personal approach. Now he writes a sentence that tells him what he wants to say about the topic as a whole. This sentence is called the ***thesis statement***. Later on Gerry will use it to write the opening of his essay.

*Because of the changes in technology, a typical day in the year 2000 will be very different from what it is now, and I am not sure that I will like all the changes.*

---

**Your Essay** 🆆🅿️

Look at the notes you have made and decide on a purpose for your essay.

PURPOSE _____

_____

_____

Choose a tone that suits your purpose and write a sentence that uses the appropriate words and states in general what you want to say about the subject.

THESIS STATEMENT _____

_____

_____

_____

---

# *Organizing Your Ideas*

*Your essay will make more sense if related ideas are grouped together.*

## WARMUP

When you know what you want to write about and are sure you have enough to say, you still need to organize the details in some way. Not all your facts, ideas, illustrations, examples, and reasons are equally important. Some are main ideas and some are subtopics. Some of the subtopics belong with one main idea; some belong with another. Some may not belong at all.

For example, look at the following items and the way they are grouped.

CELEBRATIONS
I. National Holidays
    A. July 4th
    B. Washington's Birthday
    C. Martin Luther King Day
    D. Memorial Day

II. Personal Holidays
    A. Birthdays
    B. Anniversaries
    C. Weddings
    D. Graduation

The word "Celebrations" describes all the items in the list. Then the list is divided into two main topics—"National Holidays" and "Personal Holidays." Beneath each of these is a group of subtopics that name specific holidays in each category. Could items like "Easter" and "Passover" be added to this list as it stands, or would another category have to be added?

Here is an activity to help you practice grouping related ideas together.

---

### Try It

Each list below contains three different kinds of items. One describes the general category to which all the others belong. It could be called the **theme**. Three items are **main topics**. They are not as important as the theme, but each one names a category of things or ideas. The rest of the list consists of **subtopics** that belong under one or another of the main topics. Organize each list, writing the items in the blanks provided. First find the theme, then the three main topics, then the subtopics that belong with each main topic.

| 1. bananas | cashews | snack foods |
| peanuts | bread | walnuts |
| dry cereal | apples | oranges |
| fruit | grains | crackers |
| | | nuts |

---

continued...

THEME _____

I. _____

    A. _____

    B. _____

    C. _____

II. _____

    A. _____

    B. _____

    C. _____

III. _____

    A. _____

    B. _____

    C. _____

2. laboratory work    written assignments    standardized tests
   discussions    reports    essays
   kinds of schoolwork    tests    debates
   quizzes    class activities    final exams
                                                 notes

THEME _____

I. _____

    A. _____

    B. _____

    C. _____

II. _____

    A. _____

    B. _____

    C. _____

III. _____

    A. _____

    B. _____

    C. _____

continued . . .

3. ground          steamship          bicycle
   ferry           hot-air balloon     transportation
   bus             jet plane          canoe
   air              helicopter        car
                                water

THEME _____

I. _____

    A. _____

    B. _____

    C. _____

II. _____

    A. _____

    B. _____

    C. _____

III. _____

    A. _____

    B. _____

    C. _____

## PRACTICING THE PROCESS

### Gerry's Essay

Gerry has chosen to focus his essay on what his house and his job will be like and what he will do after work for fun. He has used the brainstorming techniques he learned in Lesson 1 to come up with a list of details to include in his essay. He wrote the details in the order in which they occurred to him. Then he went back over the list and looked for ideas that went together. He put a number "1" next to all the ideas that seemed to make a group, a number "2" next to all the ideas that belonged to another group, and so on. Here is his list, with the numbers to show which details go together.

*life at home*    *1*
*office location*    *2*
*alarm clock of the future*    *1*
*transportation*    *3*
*tube connecting apartment building and office*    *3*
*life at work*    *2*
*doing things with friends*    *4*
*office equipment*    *2*
*music*    *4*

*monorail      3*
*videos instead of people      4*
*going shopping      4*
*home exercise equipment      1*
*reading      4*
*what job is like      2*
*food pellets      1*
*solar-powered cars      3*
*robot does cooking      1*

Then Gerry rewrote his list, organizing the items into main topics and subtopics. Notice that most of the main topics were on his original list. In one case, though, after he had grouped the subtopics together, he needed to add a main topic that described all the items in that group.

*LIFE AT HOME*
*alarm clock of the future*
*home exercise equipment*
*food pellets*
*robot does cooking*

*LIFE AT WORK*
*office location*
*office equipment*
*what job is like*

*TRANSPORTATION*
*tube connecting apartment building and office*
*monorail*
*solar-powered cars*

*ENTERTAINMENT*
*doing things with friends*
*going shopping*
*reading*
*music*
*videos instead of people*

---

### Your Essay [WP]

Review the brainstorming techniques that you practiced in Lesson 1. Choose one or more techniques that work well for you and use them to make a list of details to include in your essay. Write your list on a separate sheet of paper. Then look for items in your list that belong together. Some of the items may be main topics; others will be subtopics. Number the items, using the same number for items that go together.

When all the items have been numbered, copy the list below, with the items arranged in groups. Make sure each group is headed by a main topic. Add a main topic whenever you need to. It should describe all the items under it in that group.

---

continued . . .

# Arranging Ideas in Good Order

*Your essay will be easier to read if the ideas are arranged in an order that makes sense.*

## WARMUP

When ideas flow smoothly from one paragraph to the next, readers have a feeling that the writer is making sense. Deciding ahead of time what order—or **sequence**—your ideas will be arranged in is the key to smooth writing.

*Time order* is used whenever you are telling a story, describing a sequence of events, or explaining how to do something. By choosing time order you are telling your reader that it is very important which things happened first.

---

**Try It 1**

For a narrative essay on A Mountain Climbing Adventure, Todd grouped these items into main topics and subtopics. Number the main topics 1, 2, or 3 to show the order in which they should appear in the final essay. Then number the subtopics in the order you think is best.

PRACTICING AT BASE CAMP
final test
the first step—learning to use the equipment
practicing on small, nearby rocks

MAKING PLANS
sending in the application
writing away for information about a lot of camps
deciding on mountain-climbing

THE CLIMB
halfway up—slipping off the cliff
walking to the climb
resting at the top of the climb
the trip back—almost as hard

---

*Space Order* is used most often when you are describing something. Your job as a writer is to help your reader see something as a whole. If you jump around from detail to detail in no particular order, the reader will have a hard time seeing the complete picture. Putting details in space order cures the problem. You may begin your description with the thing that is farthest away and end with the thing that is nearest—or you may do the opposite. You may go from inside to outside or from outside to inside. You may also go from top to botton or bottom to top.

**Try It 2**

For a descriptive paragraph about what it is like to wake up in a mountain cabin after the first heavy snowfall of the year, Jessica listed the following details:

1. frozen water pitcher by my bedside
2. small trees completely hidden
3. such a clear day—could see for miles
4. windows half covered with snow

Use these details to complete the paragraph below. Place the number of each detail from the list above in the appropriate space.

I looked beside me and saw the _____. Something had happened during the night. Although my watch said it was 9 o'clock, there was very little light in the cabin. Then I noticed that _____. After getting dressed and pushing the door open, I stepped out into a world in which _____. Brightness surrounded me. It was _____.

**Order of Importance** is another way to organize a paragraph or an essay. You can begin with the most important happening or reason, or you can begin with the least important happening or reason and build to the most important.

Here is a paragraph that Shelly wrote, giving her reasons for learning to play the piano.

*The main reason is that I have always liked listening to piano music. One of my earliest memories is sitting on my grandmother's lap and having her hold my hand and place my fingers on the keys to play "Silent Night." Almost as important, I suppose, is that I had my mother as a built-in piano teacher. After all, she plays for all the dance schools in town and is an organist in the church. Finally, I like to sing as well as play music, and the piano lets me do both.*

Shelly used words like **the main reason** and **almost as important** to tell the reader that she had arranged her sentences in the order of most important to least important.

**Try It 3**

Rewrite Shelly's paragraph so that it ends with the most important reason for learning to play the piano. Use words that let the reader know in what direction your thought is moving. The first sentence has been written for you.

To begin with, I like to sing as well as play music, and the piano lets me do both.

_____

_____

_____

_____

_____

***General to Specific*** One of the commonest ways of arranging ideas is to go from the most general to the most specific. In this kind of arrangement the writer begins with a big idea and then gradually gets more and more specific. Here's a paragraph from Jon's paper about forests.

> *From the air all forests look pretty much alike. In the summer you see them as miles and miles of dark green carpet. If you could leave your plane and fly like a bird, you could then get close enough to see the individual trees. Then you would realize that all the trees are of different heights and that they are not the same green—some trees have lighter leaves. Then, if you could change again and be an insect on just one branch of a tree, you might see that each twig was different, too. Some twigs are longer than others and some twigs are browner than others.*

Think of using the "forest to the trees" approach whenever you are working with a big idea that contains a middle-sized idea that, in turn, contains a smaller idea.

---

**Try It 4**

Arrange the following groups of items in the way that goes from the most general to the most specific.

1. food      spaghetti      Italian cooking

   _____

2. chair      wooden objects      furniture

   _____

3. book      reading material      chapter

   _____

4. outdoor work      job choices      gardener

   _____

5. sports      baseball      team sports

   _____

6. emotion      whimper      helplessness

   _____

7. fresh fruit      health      proper diet

   _____

8. elected officials      mayors      leaders

   _____

9. nonmechanical ones      pencil      writing tools

   _____

10. violets      plants   flowers

   _____

## PRACTICING THE PROCESS

### Gerry's Essay

When Gerry looks at the list of details he has grouped, he realizes that he will probably use chronological order for his essay. Since he is describing a typical day, he will begin at the beginning—when he wakes up—go on to his work day, then describe what he does after work and when he gets home at night. He will regroup his headings and details to look like this.

*GETTING UP*
*GOING TO WORK*
*HAVING FUN AFTER WORK*

He checks his assignment to see if he has covered everything and realizes that he has left out a very important part of his thesis statement—he needs to explain what he feels about this typical day. Since he wants to describe everything first, he thinks that he will probably say how he feels at the end. He adds the word *conclusion* to his list to show this.

*GETTING UP*
*GOING TO WORK*
*HAVING FUN AFTER WORK*
*CONCLUSION*

---

### Your Essay [WP]

Look at your list of topics and decide in what order you want to arrange them. Will time order suit them best? Or will it be space order? How about order of importance or going from the general to the specific? (You may even use a mixture.)

Write down the main topics in the order you have chosen. Remember to include the ideas that are in your thesis statement.

_____

_____

_____

_____

_____

_____

# GOOD SENTENCES

The lessons in this section are different from those in the rest of the book. Instead of showing you another student's essay and helping you with part of your essay, these lessons show you some ways to make the sentences you write clearer, smoother, and more interesting. Whether you are working on a first draft or revising your essay, Good Sentences will help you with the following problems:

- Making descriptions more specific.

- Using transition and focusing words.

- Combining sentences.

- Using parallel structures.

- Avoiding repetition.

# Specific Words

*Using specific words makes your writing more interesting.*

Read these sentences. Then answer the questions that follow.

1. The final exam will be soon.
2. The weather forecaster said it would be a nice day.
3. Lou went to get his things.

- What day is the final exam?
- Should you wear a sweater?
- Will Lou need help in carrying his things?

There is no way you can answer the questions because you do not have enough information. Now see what happens when you replace one word in each sentence.

1. The final exam will be Tuesday.
2. The weather forecaster said it would be warm and sunny.
3. Lou went to get the trunkful of dishes.

Words like **soon**, **nice**, and **things** that do not contain specific information are called **vague**. The word **vague** comes from a Latin word meaning "to wander" or "to roam," and that is exactly what these words do. They never quite get to the point. Vague words are used a lot in conversation, usually because the people who are talking know pretty much what they are talking about. In Sentence 3, for example, you can imagine a friend of Lou's explaining to another friend why Lou will be a little late.

It is important to use specific words in writing because your reader has no other way of knowing what you are talking about and how you feel about something. Remember, when you write, the words alone carry the entire message. If you want someone to realize that you were so disappointed at losing the game that you thought you would give up basketball, you have to say exactly that. Writing a sentence like **Losing the game was pretty bad** is not specific enough.

## Practice 1

In the sentences below, the underlined words are too vague. Make each sentence more specific by substituting words from the list below. Write your revised sentences.

| | | |
|---|---|---|
| fresh | flattering | scary |
| weights | poured | enormous |
| exciting | slithered | prizewinning |
| | | blizzard |

1. A black snake <u>moved</u> through the grass.

_____

2. The waters of the spring flood <u>came</u> into the house.

_____

3. The <u>storm</u> of 1978 left thousands of people stranded.

_____

4. The visitors from New Guinea stared at the <u>big</u> skyscraper.

_____

5. I'd like a <u>nice</u> loaf of Italian bread.

_____

6. That's a <u>nice</u> dress.

_____

7. *The Mystery of No Shoes* is a <u>good</u> book.

_____

8. Ralph had an <u>interesting</u> time at the World's Fair.

_____

9. The gallery owner showed us a <u>good</u> painting.

_____

10. Let's lift a few <u>things</u>.

_____

Another way to make your writing more interesting is to use **synonyms**. A synonym is a word that means almost the same thing as another word. Here are some synonyms you are probably already familiar with.

*fix* ............*repair*
*cold* .........*icy*

You can use a regular dictionary or a dictionary of synonyms to find the word you want.

## Practice 2

Match the word in Column A with a synonym in Column B.

| A | B |
|---|---|
| _____ prize | 1. weak |
| _____ shine | 2. equal |
| _____ feeble | 3. knowledge |
| _____ learning | 4. catch |
| _____ order | 5. award |
| _____ forgetful | 6. innocent |
| _____ identical | 7. command |
| _____ capture | 8. insult |
| _____ harmless | 9. glitter |
| _____ offend | 10. absentminded |

Although synonyms mean almost the same thing, they are different enough to make you think twice before you substitute one word for another. Here are three synonyms that describe some-one's feelings after a day of work.

*fatigued*      *tired*      *worn out*

Each of these words expresses a different idea about the feeling. We might think that someone who is fatigued has probably not worked as hard as someone who is tired. Probably neither has worked as hard as the person who is worn out. These words are different because they have different **connotations**—or different associations in our minds. Good writers are always aware of how a word is used before they use it.

## Practice 3

Use the words from Practice 2 to complete each sentence. Think about the associations that your mind attaches to each word before you select it.

1. We've been sitting at this table for fifteen minutes and no one has taken our

   _____.

2. Shara has read twenty books about Lincoln. Her _____ of Civil War

   history is extraordinary.

3. Mo and Jo are _____ twins.

4. Todd has never liked _____ tea or coffee.

5. How can you tell if a snake is _____?

# Transition and Focusing Words

*Good writers emphasize important ideas.*
*Good writers make connections between ideas.*

Read the two paragraphs below. How are they different from each other? What do the words in dark type add to paragraph II? Are the relationships between ideas clearer?

I      We didn't notice anything. It began to occur to us that something was the matter. We weren't sure what had happened, we didn't know what to do to fix it. We were afraid of making it worse.

II      We didn't notice anything **at first**. **Then** it began to occur to us that something was the matter. **Since** we weren't sure what had happened, **however**, we didn't know what to do to fix it. **Besides**, we were afraid of making it worse.

No matter what you write—whether you are describing something, explaining something, or making an argument—you want the reader to be able to follow you. You cannot just put down your ideas or observations without some signals that let the reader know what is coming next. Words like **then**, **here**, **so**, **because**, **although**, **for instance**, and **for these reasons** tell the reader the following kinds of things:

- This is what I plan to discuss.
- This is what happened first.
- This is how these two ideas are connected.
- Here is an example.
- This is important.
- Now I have finished.

These words provide *transitions*, or make connections, between sentences and paragraphs. They also help the reader *focus* on particular ideas or pieces of information. Transition and focusing words help the reader see what your main points are and how the pieces of your essay are related.

---

### Practice 1

There are many kinds of transition and focusing words. Some of them are given below. They are grouped to show how they can be used in sentences. Following each group is a practice sentence. Choose a transition or focusing word (or group of words) to complete the sentence and write it in the blank. (Notice that in some cases there are several possible choices.)

---

continued...

1. *Words used to add or emphasize ideas, information, or examples:*

   for example, for instance, in addition, in other words, furthermore, also, specifically, besides, moreover, further, again, in the first place, equally important, as well, in fact, such as, such . . . , this . . . , that . . . , these . . . , those . . .

   Georgia's ideas—_____, her plan for recycling peanut shells—are sometimes difficult to carry out.

2. *Words used to show time order:*

   first, second, next, then, now, last, finally, meanwhile, later, earlier, before, after, at the same time, during

   _____ we read the report, we will be ready to tell you what we think of it.

3. *Words used to show space order:*

   above, below, left, right, inside, outside, on top of, underneath, next to, in front, behind, beyond, near, far, in, on, under

   _____ the desk is a neatly lettered sign that says "Genius at work."

4. *Words used to show order of importance:*

   first, last, next, then, nearly, in the first place, moreover, furthermore, most important, equally important, less important, so, therefore, consequently

   Mendoza's theory, _____, is the most original idea to be published in the last ten years.

5. *Words used to compare or contrast ideas:*

   however, though, even though, although, on the other hand, yet, nevertheless, conversely, as opposed to, rather than, in spite of, compared to, similarly, in the same way, as well as, likewise

   During the past week, _____, new evidence has come to our attention.

6. *Words used to show cause and effect:*

   since, as, because (of), due to, so, therefore, then, consequently, as a result (of), in effect, for this reason, accordingly

   _____, Professor Pirenza no longer knows what to believe.

7. *Words used to summarize or conclude:*

   briefly, to summarize, to sum up, in short, for these reasons, in conclusion, to conclude, as you can see, in other words, in any case, on the whole, undoubtedly, after all

   The result, _____, is confusion and uncertainty for everyone involved in the project.

## Practice 2

The following two paragraphs need to have transition and focusing words added to them. Fill each blank with the word or group of words from the list below that makes the most sense.

[1] _____, scientists have known about the loud, trumpeting sounds elephants make to communicate. Now, [2] _____, they have begun to study another form of elephant communication. Elephants have a spot on their forehead that vibrates when they bellow or growl. It vibrates at other times [3] _____. The scientists cannot hear anything, [4] _____ they are convinced that the elephants are producing sounds too low for human ears.

The existence of [5] _____ low-frequency sounds could explain some of the mysteries of elephant communication. [6] _____, it would explain how elephants communicate over long distances, [7] _____ low-frequency sounds travel much farther than high-frequency sounds. This sort of complex communication system might [8] _____ explain how elephants are able to organize their society.

| | | |
|---|---|---|
| but | during | consequently |
| nearly | however | for a long time |
| for example | such | since |
| as well | also | rather than |

# Combining Sentences–A

*Effective sentences often combine several ideas.*

Good writing uses both short sentences and long ones. One kind of sentence is not necessarily better than the other. However, writing that uses only one kind—short sentences only or long sentences only—is often monotonous or difficut to read.

> This is an example. It shows one kind of writing. This kind of writing uses short sentences. It does not use long sentences. It is not very interesting. All the sentences sound alike. The reader starts to fall asleep.

> This is another example of writing that uses only one kind of sentence—in this case, long sentences—to the exclusion of everything else. What you, the reader, will discover, however, is that a long sentence, like a short sentence, can sometimes be too much of a good thing, and that after a while, the reader, though not asleep, may be thoroughly confused.

You need practice in order to use both short sentences and long sentences effectively. In this lesson and the next few lessons, you will be working with combining ideas into longer sentences. Later on, you will also work on eliminating unnecessary words and sentences.

When you combine ideas, you do not need to repeat all the words in the original sentences. Combining usually means condensing to some extent. It can also mean changing the structure, or the way the sentence is put together. Notice, for example, how the following sentences are changed when they are combined.

> Rex is our dog. He lay on the rug. His eyes were closed. His nose was twitching.
> Our dog Rex lay on the rug with his eyes closed and his nose twitching.

The first activity in each of these lessons consists of multiple-choice questions to give you practice with the kinds of questions sometimes used in tests of writing. The second activity gives you a chance to write your own sentences.

---

**Practice 1**

Circle the letter of the sentence that shows the best way to combine each group of ideas.

*Example:*    Justin ran up the stairs. Justin tripped on a board. The board was loose.
        a. Justin ran up the stairs, and he tripped on a board, and it was loose.
        b. Running up the stairs, Justin tripped on a loose board.
        c. There was a loose board in the stairs, and Justin tripped on it while he was running up them.
        d. Justin tripped on a board when he was running up the stairs because it was loose.

continued . . .

1. Myra prepared for the test. The test was the next day. Myra frowned in concentration.
   a. There was a test the next day, and Myra prepared for it, frowning in concentration.
   b. The test was the next day, and Myra was preparing for it, and she frowned in concentration.
   c. Myra prepared for the test, and she frowned in concentration, and it was the next day.
   d. Preparing for the test the next day, Myra frowned in concentration.

2. Lester prefers tacos. He likes them with chopped onion. He also likes grated cheese on them.
   a. Lester prefers tacos, and he likes them with chopped onion and also with grated cheese.
   b. Lester likes tacos, and he likes chopped onion, and he likes grated cheese.
   c. Lester prefers tacos with chopped onion and grated cheese.
   d. Lester likes chopped onion and grated cheese.

3. We took our time. We ambled home. We walked along Greene Street.
   a. Taking our time, we ambled home along Greene Street.
   b. Because we walked along Greene Street and took our time, we ambled home.
   c. We took our time, and we ambled home, and we walked along Greene Street.
   d. Taking our time and ambling and walking along Greene Street, we went home.

4. B.J. was surprised. She had just heard something. It was about her old friend T.Y. It was good news.
   a. B.J. was surprised because she had just heard something, and it was good news about her old friend T.Y.
   b. B.J. had just heard some good news, and it surprised her, and it was about her old friend T.Y.
   c. B.J. was surprised to hear good news about her old friend T.Y.
   d. B.J. was surprised, and she had just had some good news, and it was about her old friend T.Y.

5. Edith found a wallet. It was red. There was a driver's license in it.
   a. There was a driver's license in the wallet that Edith found, and it was red.
   b. Edith found a red wallet with a driver's license in it.
   c. Edith found a wallet with a driver's license in it.
   d. Edith found a wallet, and it was red, and it had a driver's license in it.

## Practice 2

Write a new sentence that combines each group of ideas below. Remember that you do not have to repeat every word when you combine sentences.

**Example:** Marietta walked down the street. Marietta ignored the people she saw. They were homeless.

*Walking down the street, Marietta ignored the homeless people she saw.*

1. Pudge barked. He barked at the top of his lungs. Pudge raced to the front door.

   _____

   _____

2. Franklin bought a pair of sneakers. They were black. They had purple laces.

   _____

   _____

3. Angie smiled at the crowd. The crowd was in the auditorium. Angie began to read her speech.

   _____

   _____

4. Marva was happy. She had heard something. It was about the new contract. The union had just signed it.

   _____

   _____

5. Carl made a sandwich. It was huge. It had tomatoes in it. It also had sardines in it.

   _____

   _____

# Combining Sentences–B

*When ideas are combined, words like **since** and **although** can show the relationships between them.*

When ideas are combined, they can express a variety of relationships.

cause and effect: Mark screamed **because** his sister kicked him.

time: It rained **while** you were away.

contradiction: **Although** Nancy works hard, she never quite catches up.

equality: The dog howled, **and** the cat yowled.

Words used to show these relationships include the following:

| | | |
|---|---|---|
| after | before | or |
| although | but | since |
| and | even though | so |
| as | for | when |
| as soon as | however | while |
| because | in order to | |

When you combine ideas, it is important to make the new sentence as concise, or condensed, as possible. At the same time, you want to express the relationship between the ideas clearly. For example, compare these two ways of combining ideas:

Jeannette went home. First she went to the bank, though. She deposited her paycheck.

    a. Jeannette went to the bank and deposited her paycheck, and then she went home.

    b. Before going home, Jeannette went to the bank to deposit her paycheck.

Which is more concise? Which expresses the relationship between the ideas more clearly?

Notice that you could also express the relationship between these ideas in the following way:

After going to the bank to deposit her paycheck, Jeannette went home.

The way you choose depends on what you want to emphasize.

## Practice 1

Circle the letter of the sentence that shows the best way to combine each group of ideas.

**Example:**   George sets up the chairs for the meeting. He whistles at the same time.
a. Although George whistles, he sets up the chairs for the meeting.
(b.) George whistles while he sets up the chairs for the meeting.
c. George sets up the chairs for the meeting, so he whistles.
d. George whistles, but he sets up the chairs for the meeting.

1. Chris managed to leave on time. He got up late.
a. Since Chris got up late, he managed to leave on time.
b. Chris managed to leave on time, and he got up late.
c. Chris managed to leave on time, even though he got up late.
d. Because Chris managed to leave on time, he got up late.

2. Ida wanted to fix the window. The window was broken. She needed a new pane of glass.
a. In order to fix the broken window, Ida needed a new pane of glass.
b. The window was broken, so Ida wanted to fix it, and she needed a new pane of glass.
c. Because she fixed the broken window, Ida needed a new pane of glass.
d. Although the window was broken, Ida needed a new pane of glass to fix it.

3. Monica looks longingly into the bakery window. She is hungry.
a. Because Monica looks longingly into the bakery window, she is hungry.
b. Monica looks longingly into the bakery window although she is hungry.
c. Monica is hungry, but she looks longingly into the bakery window.
d. Monica looks longingly into the bakery window because she is hungry.

4. The wind howled more fiercely. We pulled the blankets around us.
a. We pulled the blankets around us, and the wind howled more fiercely.
b. Although the wind howled more fiercely, we pulled the blankets around us.
c. As the wind howled more fiercely, we pulled the blankets around us.
d. We pulled the blankets around us, but the wind howled more fiercely.

5. Richard received the assignment. The assignment was due Wednesday. He began to work on it right away.
a. Richard received the assignment and began to work on it right away, and it was due Wednesday.
b. As soon as he received it, Richard began to work on the assignment that was due Wednesday.
c. Because Richard received the assignment that was due Wednesday, he began to work on it right away.
d. When Richard received the assignment, he began to work on it, but it was due Wednesday.

## Practice 2

Write a new sentence that combines each group of ideas below. Use the word given to connect the ideas. Remember that you do not have to repeat every word when you combine sentences.

**Example:**  Everyone seemed to be there. George decided to begin the meeting. (Use **since**.)

*Since everyone seemed to be there, George decided to begin the meeting.*

1. It rained and Sheila forgot the picnic basket. Stanley had a good time anyway. (Use **although**.)

   _____

   _____

2. The temperature is 20 degrees and snow is falling. The calendar says it is spring. (Use **but**.)

   _____

   _____

3. No one wants to admit defeat yet. There are still two minutes left to play. (Use **because**.)

   _____

   _____

4. Eileen was tiptoeing down the stairs. A light suddenly went on in the hallway. (Use **as**.)

   _____

   _____

5. The kingdom was bankrupt. The prince and princess went out to look for jobs. (Use **so**.)

   _____

   _____

# Parallelism

*Good writers write balanced sentences.*

Which of these sentences is easier to remember? Read both sentences softly to yourself. Then cover them with a piece of paper and say them again.

1. Marta liked to dance, ice-skate, and swim.

2. Marta liked to dance, going ice-skating, and she could swim.

Sentence 1 is easier for most people to remember because the words that end the sentence—the words that follow **to**—all have the same structure. That means, too, that they have a similar rhythm. Poets and musicians and writers all know that words with the same rhythm stay longer in your mind.

In the second sentence the words that follow **to** do not have a similar structure. There is no set rhythm for your mind to follow. The sentence is not as smooth and not as easy to remember.

Choosing words or groups of words that have the same structure is a device that writers use to make their words **memorable**—easy to remember. The name for this technique is **parallelism**. Writers use parallelism when they want to show that the ideas they are discussing are related. Here are some other examples of parallelism, with the parallel structures printed in dark type.

1. Ned acted as **producer**, **director**, and **writer** on the film.

2. One critic said that both **the actor who played the gunfighter** and **the actor who played the Navaho chief** should be nominated for Oscars.

3. Although she wanted to see the movie, Joni didn't know **when she could go** or **how she could get there**.

4. By **getting a job** and **saving her money**, Marca paid for acting lessons.

5. The film director was always asking her crew **to look for the best shot**, **to wait for the best shot**, and **to take the best shot**.

## Practice 1

Complete each sentence with the item that has a structure **parallel** to the parts of the sentence printed in dark type. Circle the letter of the item.

1. Chris planned to study **TV production**, **photography** and _____.
   a. film making
   b. making films
   c. how to make a film
   d. all about films

2. In choosing an actor for the lead, Chris wanted someone who knew how to **ride a horse**, **use a rifle**, and even _____.
   a. building a log cabin
   b. could build a log cabin
   c. build a log cabin
   d. all about log cabins

3. The studio asked the director if he could finish the film without **waiting an extra day** _____.
   a. and not doing any more scene writing
   b. or writing another scene
   c. and no more scenes, either
   d. or scene-writing anymore

4. Chris wanted a movie **that made people cry half the time** and _____.
   a. that they enjoyed too
   b. that they laughed at as well
   c. that they thought it was funny too
   d. that made them laugh the other half

5. Someone who really likes Westerns, horses, and _____ should see this film.
   a. to get a look at the mountains
   b. seeing mountains
   c. mountain scenery
   d. mountains

**Practice 2**

Each sentence below has an underlined portion that may be correct or incorrect. If you think the underlined portion is correct, circle a. If you think it is incorrect, circle the letter of the answer you believe is correct.

1. In home economics, Sean learned how to boil an egg, making French toast, and bake bread.
   a. making French toast
   b. French toasting
   c. make French toast
   d. all about French toast

2. The senator said that there would be more jobs, less pollution, and lowering taxes.
   a. lowering taxes
   b. it would make taxes lower
   c. lower taxes
   d. taxes would be lower

3. To make strawberry shortcake, you need strawberries, whipped cream, and to bake some biscuits
   a. to bake some biscuits
   b. baking biscuits
   c. also to bake some biscuits
   d. biscuits

4. The interviewer was impressed by Tom's experience in selling potholders and also he was enthusiastic about the job.
   a. also he was enthusiastic about the job
   b. his enthusiasm about the job
   c. he showed enthusiasm about the job
   d. he seemed enthusiastic about the job

5. The day of the class picnic was hot and there was a lot of sun.
   a. there was a lot of sun
   b. filled with sun
   c. there was no rain
   d. sunny

## GOOD SENTENCES 6:

# *Avoiding Repetition*

*Good writers avoid repeating words and ideas unnecessarily.*

Read the two pairs of examples below. How are example I and II different from each other? Are the words in dark type in example I necessary? Are any ideas lost when these words are removed in example II?

> I   The most serious mistake I ever made is something that turned out to be funny. ***It was a mistake I thought was serious but it really was something funny.***
>
> II   The most serious mistake I ever made is something that turned out to be funny.

> I   That is how I learned that **some disasters turn out different from the way they seem at first.** Not every disaster is what it seems to be.
>
> II   That is how I learned that not every disaster is what it seems to be.

Unnecessary repetition of ideas is a trap that is easy to fall into, especially in the introduction or conclusion of an essay. When you are making a general statement or summing up your ideas, you sometimes say the same thing more often than you need to. You may be unsure of what you want to say or how you want to say it. Without planning to, you may try out your ideas in several ways in order to discover the best way of expressing yourself.

You can keep from repeating ideas by asking yourself whether a sentence adds anything new:

> I   Many people began moving west in 1848. 1848 was the beginning of a great westward movement.
>
> II   1848 was the beginning of a great westward movement.

You can also combine or rearrange ideas to avoid repetition:

> I   There are many explanations of why people decided to move west. The reasons that people decided to move west are numerous.
>
> II   There are many reasons that people decided to go out west.

> I   The author describes the westward movement of 1848, when the pioneers moved west.
>
> II   The author describes the westward movement of the pioneers in 1848.

**Practice 1**

Rewrite each sentence or pair of sentences to avoid repeating ideas. Remember that you can just take out an entire sentence in some cases. In other cases, you will need to combine or rearrange ideas in addition to taking them out. There is more than one way to rewrite each item.

1. I will always remember the day I got my first set of drums. How could I forget the day I got my first drum set?

   _____

   _____

2. No one would ever figure out why Uncle George chose to come out of hiding just then. We never knew why he chose to come out of hiding at that moment.

   _____

   _____

3. This book describes the Industrial Revolution in America, when America had the Industrial Revolution in the nineteenth century.

   _____

   _____

4. It is still difficult for me to believe that all this really happened. I still can't believe that all these events occurred.

   _____

   _____

5. These facts explain why today is called "The Information Age," which is the age we live in.

   _____

   _____

6. The Great Depression was a difficult time to live in. Life was very hard during the Great Depression.

   _____

   _____

Now look at the following examples. How are they different from each other? How have the words in dark type been changed?

I   Luis works in a very **modern** factory. The building is new and **modern**, and it has all the most **modern** equipment.

II   Luis works in a very modern factory. The building is new, and it has all the most up-to-date equipment.

Sometimes you repeat individual words unnecessarily, especially when you are adding supporting details to the main idea. If your main idea is that the factory is modern, you want the details to show that the factory is modern. The trick is not to keep repeating the word **modern**. Sometimes you can take it out altogether. Sometimes you need to find a **synonym** as a substitute.

---

**Practice 2**

Rewrite each group of sentences to avoid repeating words. Remember that you can either take out a repeated word or find a synonym to use instead. There is more than one way to rewrite each item.

1. I remember August 14 best of all because it was a perfect day. The weather was sunny and perfect, and the beach looked perfect as we stepped onto the sand.

   _____

   _____

   _____

2. A terrible disaster occurred. It is hard to imagine anything more terrible. Robert had made a terrible mistake.

   _____

   _____

   _____

3. Next year will be very important. It will be filled with important decisions. The important steps I take then will affect the rest of my life.

   _____

   _____

   _____

4. This article contains good ideas for saving money. It explains a good, easy way to find bargains when you shop. It also has some good tips on putting your money to work for you.

   _____

   _____

   _____

---

# WRITING

Writing is the step in which you put a first draft of your essay down on paper. It is the shortest section in this book, consisting of just the following lessons:

- Writing the opening of the essay.

- Adding on paragraphs.

- Writing the closing of the essay.

In reality, writing is more like a spiral than like a straight line. It includes both prewriting and revising. You might start by turning your lists, questions, and notes into sentences. In the middle of this process, however, you might decide to brainstorm new ideas in order to add or change something. As you write, you might also change your mind about your choice of words or the order in which you have arranged ideas. In this case, you might revise as you write.

Although the techniques of prewriting and revising are often used in the writing stage, in this book they are introduced separately so that you can practice them individually.

You will write a first draft in this part of the book. You will not have finished writing, though, until you revise and edit what you have written.

# *Writing the First Paragraph*

*Knowing what your main idea is helps you begin your first paragraph.*

## WARMUP

A paragraph is a group of sentences that focuses on one main idea. Often a paragraph begins with a *topic sentence* that states this general idea. The topic sentence is a *focusing* sentence that lets the reader know right away what the paragraph is going to be about. Each of the remaining sentences adds a detail or gives an example or a reason that makes the idea contained in the topic sentence more real or more believable.

Nina wrote a descriptive paragraph about her first part-time job.

> [1] The first day on a new job can be a real disaster. [2] You have to learn so many new things that you often forget the things you already know. [3] Answering a telephone, which every teenager knows how to do very well, becomes impossible when the phone has five different number buttons as well as a hold button. [4] When you finally do push the right button, you realize that saying, ''Good morning. This is Riddle's Packing,'' is a lot harder than saying, ''Hi.'' [5] To make matters worse, getting coffee for all the bosses means not only figuring out how to work another new machine but also how to carry three cups without spilling a drop.

Sentence 1: This is the topic sentence. It focuses on the general idea that starting a new job is never easy. Because Nina exaggerates by calling it a "real disaster," the reader knows right away that this paragraph is meant to be humorous.

Sentence 2: This sentence explains in what way the first day can be a problem—learning new things can make you forget what you know.

Sentence 3: This sentence gives a detail that makes the general statements real and believable.

Sentence 4: This sentence adds an example that further explains the detail in Sentence 3.

Sentence 5: Another detail is added.

In Nina's paragraph all the sentences fit together to create a complete picture in the reader's mind.

## Try It 1

Read the paragraph below and decide which of the sentences that follow it would make the best topic sentence. Choose the sentence that sums up all the other sentences.

First of all, I hadn't even known that there was going to be a contest. Fortunately, one of my friends had seen the announcement in the bike store window and told me about it. The prize was $25 for the best color poster about bicycle safety. The deadline was in two days, and, to make matters worse, I had to study for exams. Would I have time to do a good job? I didn't think I had time to do anything at all, but Fred told me that I was the best artist he knew. I felt I had to try. When exams were over, I worked most of the night just getting the idea. Then, the next day, with only two hours until the deadline, I finished the poster.

_____ a. Designing a poster can be a lot of hard work.

_____ b. Winning the poster contest was something that almost didn't happen.

_____ c. Where would I be without Fred?

Earlier in this book, you practiced writing a thesis statement that told what the main idea of your essay was going to be. When you write the first draft of your essay, you can turn the thesis statement into the topic sentence of the first paragraph. You can also use just part of it at the beginning and save the rest.

## Try It 2

Here are the main groups and the thesis statement that Karen used for her essay.

MEMORIES OF FORMER LIFE
COMING TO AMERICA
LEARNING TO BE A CITIZEN OF THE UNITED STATES

THESIS STATEMENT: *I had mixed-up feelings on the day I became a citizen because part of me was sad about leaving behind my old life in the Philippines and part of me was very glad that my family was in America and that I would grow up here.*

Which of the following sentences would make a good topic sentence for her first paragraph? Choose the one that fits the general idea of the essay and the first paragraph, which is about Karen's memories of the Philippines.

_____ a. Becoming an American citizen was the happiest day of my life.

_____ b. Although I was proud and happy about becoming a United States citizen, I couldn't help remembering my childhood in the Philippines.

_____ c. I was glad that my family had decided to come to America and that I was becoming a citizen.

## PRACTICING THE PROCESS

### Gerry's Essay

Gerry looks at the thesis statement he wrote for his essay.

*Because of the changes in technology, a typical day in the year 2000 will be different from what it is now, and I am not sure that I will like all the changes.*

Since he has already decided that his essay will have a conclusion that tells how he feels about his future life, he uses only part of his thesis statement to begin his first paragraph.

This is Gerry's first paragraph. It is a first draft, which means that not all the words and sentences are written exactly the way he would like them. It also means that not all the spelling and punctuation is correct. Gerry's teacher has told him not to worry about that in a first draft. The important thing is to start writing.

```
Because of the changes in technology, a typical day in the year 2000
will be very different from what it is now. For one thing, mornings
begin in a different way. There are'nt any alarm clocks anymore. A
special device wakes me up. It shakes me out of bed and shakes me onto
the floor. The closet door opens automatically, and the exercise
equipmnet comes out. The Robot—Cook begins heating the food pel-
lets for breakfast.
```

---

**Your Essay** 📝

Read your thesis statement. Then look at your list of main ideas and details. On a separate piece of paper, write the first paragraph with a topic sentence that uses some of the words and ideas you put in the thesis statement. Don't worry about all the words and spellings at this time. You will have plenty of chances to make improvements when you revise. Remember to save your paper.

---

**THINK ABOUT** Gerry's first paragraph. What changes do you think he might want to make when he starts to revise his essay?

# Adding on Paragraphs

*Knowing how your main ideas are related helps you connect the paragraphs in your essay.*

## WARMUP

You have learned about connecting the ideas in a paragraph. When you write more than one paragraph, you also need to connect the paragraphs. The order in which you have arranged the ideas in your essay can sometimes help you decide what kinds of connections to make between paragraphs.

Daniel, for example, was writing about the time he cooked dinner for the whole family. The details in his essay were arranged in time order. Notice the words he used to connect the first and second paragraphs.

> *. . . There were more steps to this job than I realized. You can't just cook some stuff and call it dinner. What if you decide to make salad and find out in the middle that there isn't any lettuce?* **You have to get organized first.**
>
> **I began by making a list of what I planned to cook.** *I checked to see what I needed to buy. . . .*

Daniel ended his first paragraph by suggesting what he would describe next—getting organized. Then he began his second paragraph by saying what he did first to get organized—"I began by making a list." The word **began** also tells the reader that other steps will follow this one.

Margie was writing about a surprise party that backfired. She compared the carefully made plans to what actually happened. Notice how this way of arranging the ideas in her essay also gave her a way to connect the paragraphs.

> *. . . Everyone would arrive at seven. We would all hide in the kitchen with the lights out until the doorbell rang twice. That would be the signal that Peter had arrived with Mom and Dad. We would get ready to jump out and yell "Surprise," and the party would begin.* **It seemed so easy. Nothing could go wrong.**
>
> **There was one detail we had overlooked, though.** *We had forgotten that Peter couldn't go anywhere without getting lost. . . .*

Margie wanted to contrast their belief that all was going well with the disaster that actually occurred. She prepared for the contrast by emphasizing how thorough all the arrangements had been and how easy it seemed to make everything work. Then, in the first sentence of the next paragraph, she told her readers to expect a contradiction. The information that a detail had been overlooked and the word **though** are hints that something different is coming.

Another way to connect paragraphs is to repeat a detail or refer to an idea in an earlier paragraph. That is what Tina did in this essay about a dream come true.

*... It's hard to say what I wanted most. Of course, I dreamed of being famous. I loved to act and hoped that some day I could do more than be in a school play. I wanted to make money, too, so that I could afford to go to college. Just as strong was my wish to get out of Plainsville. I wanted to travel and meet exciting people.*

***Then suddenly one day it looked as though all these wishes and dreams might come true.** I was being given a chance to audition for a movie. . . .*

By introducing her second paragraph with the words **all these wishes and dreams**, Tina made it clear that she was referring to the wishes and dreams she described in the first paragraph. She not only repeated the words **wish** and **dream**, she used **all these** to point out which wishes and dreams she meant.

---

**Try It**

Add sentences to connect each pair of paragraphs below. Follow the instructions about what to add and where to put it.

1. Add a sentence to the end of paragraph 1 that indicates to the reader that a list of suggestions is coming. Add a sentence at the beginning of paragraph 2 that says that making a list is the first step.

. . . Finding a summer job isn't always easy, especially if you're not old enough to drive. There is a lot of competition and not very many jobs. You have to know where to look for possible jobs, and you have to know how to make yourself look good. _____

_____

_____

_____

Think of every job you've ever done—paid work or volunteer work—and write it down. . . .

2. Add a sentence at the end of paragraph 1 that emphasizes how great the trip should have been. Add a sentence at the beginning of paragraph 2 that contrasts what the writer expected with the way things actually turned out.

. . . My parents thought that I would enjoy going to St. Louis by myself. I would have a chance to be away from them for awhile and to be on my own. Also, this would be a good opportunity to get to know my aunt and uncle and cousins better. My cousin Matt was exactly my age, so I would have somebody to go places and do things with. _____

_____

_____

_____

The whole time I was there, I don't think Matt talked to me more than twice. . . .

continued . . .

3. Add a sentence at the beginning of paragraph 2 that emphasizes the idea that every dog has a different behavior pattern. It should also introduce the idea that every dog needs to be trained in a different way.

. . . Some dogs obey because they're very timid, and they're afraid of what might happen to them if they don't obey. Some dogs are just so eager to please human beings that they will do anything you ask them to. Some dogs just happen to do what you want them to, and you can fool them into thinking you had something to do with it.

_____

_____

_____

Fortunately, there are dozens of theories of dog training. . . .

## PRACTICING THE PROCESS

### Gerry's Essay

To continue his essay, Gerry looks at the list of details he organized in prewriting and sees that the next two subtopics are "Going to Work" and "Having Fun After Work." These will be the next two paragraphs of his essay.

Here is his list of details and the two paragraphs he added to his essay. Notice how he changed his notes into sentences and how he connected the two paragraphs.

GOING TO WORK
office location
tube connecting apartment building and office
solar-powered cars
office equipment
what job is like

HAVING FUN AFTER WORK
doing things with friends
going shopping
monorail
music
videos
reading

*Getting to work is very easy. No one needs a car. Right outside the door is a moving walkway that takes me to a soler-powered transporter. Lots of things in the year 2000 use solar energy. Even my food is cooked by the sun. Anyway, it travels through the tube that connects all the buildings in this area and stops right at my office. I have the same job as everyone else I know. I feed information into a huge computer that runs the city. Nobody likes this work but there are no other kinds of jobs anymore. Fortunately, though, we only have to work for four hours a day, and then we can do what we want.*

*Some nights we ride the monorail around the mall to look at the lifelike robots. They demonstrate the sports equipment. On weekends we go to Synthesizer concerts. There aren't any live musicians, but we see 3-D videos while we listen to the music. Sometimes, though, what I like best is just to go home and spend the evening reading. Sometimes an evening of reading is what I prefer to do. I don't turn on any machines. I just read from a real book, not a computer.*

---

**Your Essay** [WP]

On the paper on which you have written your first paragraph, write everything but the last paragraph of your essay. Use the list of subtopics and details from your prewriting notes. You may be adding one, two, or three paragraphs to the paragraph you have already written. The length of your essay will depend on how many subtopics and details you include. Don't worry about all the words and spellings at this time. You will have plenty of chances to change things when you revise. Remember to save your paper.

---

**THINK ABOUT** the middle paragraphs of Gerry's essay. What changes do you think Gerry might want to make when he starts to revise his essay?

*WRITING 3:*

# *Writing the Conclusion*

*A good ending tells what you think about the topic.*

## WARMUP

Writing a good essay means more than just writing good sentences. It means more than including all the details you listed in the prewriting step. It even means more than using all the right words correctly spelled.

Writing a good essay means having an idea about something and putting it into words for someone else to understand. The most convincing ideas flow naturally from the details you have chosen to write about.

For an essay on career choice, Frankie had gathered these details and written a thesis statement.

> *an exciting job*
> *I like writing*
> *not a nine to five job*
> *can be dangerous—but that's OK*
> *learn all about life*
> *get to go everywhere*
> *solving mysteries is challenging*
> *being "in" on things*
> *I can observe dangerous things without really getting hurt*
>
> THESIS STATEMENT: *Because it is the most exciting job I know and because I like to write, I want to become a crime reporter for a newspaper.*

Her first paragraph began with the following topic sentence:

```
The one writing job that promises excitement is the writing job I

want to have--crime reporting.
```

The rest of the paragraph gave examples that showed how exciting the job of crime reporter was. In the next two paragraphs Frankie described some of the daily tasks of the crime reporter—including trying to solve mysteries. She also wrote about the dangers involved, for example, when a reporter is following a gangland story very closely. Now she needed to finish her essay with a paragraph that explained how she felt or what she thought about what she had told the reader. This is what she decided to write about in the final paragraph.

```
The purpose of the final paragraph will be to explain to the reader

that, for me, being a crime reporter lets me have excitement, but it

also gives me the advantage of having a regular job. Also, as a
```

writer I get to observe without actually taking part. A police officer is on the firing line. A writer is off to the side.

Now suppose that Frankie decided that the advantage to being a crime reporter is that you really learn a lot about life. She would have written a purpose statement that looked like this.

The purpose of the final paragraph will be to explain to the reader that in addition to the excitement that goes with the job there is the exciting feeling that I'm really learning a lot about life. I get to see the worst and the best. I get to observe life and death situations. I'm sort of like a soldier, except that my own life isn't on the line. However, I get to try to answer some of the big questions about life and to describe it to others in my writing.

---

**Try It 1**

Read the following paragraph. Pick the sentence that you think makes the best conclusion. Write it in the blank.

The clam bar and the hot dog stand at the beach were boarded up. The lifeguard station was empty—even the lifeboat was put in drydock. A few young children played on the swings, but no more sand castles were being built because the sand at the water's edge was now too cold. _____

_____

1. Summer was definitely over.
2. Why was I so unhappy?
3. I could hardly wait to get back home.

---

**Try It 2**

Read the following lists of details used in an essay about ice-skating. Think about how the details in column **A** make you feel. Then pick the sentence that you might use in the final paragraph of an essay that contained these details. Write **A** next to it. Next, read column **B**. Notice that there are additional details. Then pick a sentence that you might use in the final paragraph of an essay that contained these details. Write **B** next to it. Remember that the conclusion has to flow from the details.

continued . . .

**A**
scared
ankles turning in
don't want to lift my feet
crash—the ice is hard!
how long does it take?
crash again—hurts in the same
   place
other people dance—I can't
   even walk on ice

**B**
scared
ankles turning in
don't want to lift my feet
crash—the ice is hard!
how long does it take?
crash again—hurts in the same
   place
other people dance—I can't even
   walk on ice
friends make me stick to it
good coaching
skating backwards is great
hockey stops are fun
my first medal

_____ 1. Learning to ice-skate took more time than I thought it would, but it was worth it.

_____ 2. Although I hadn't expected much the first time I tried to ice-skate, I certainly hadn't expected it to be as bad as it was.

_____ 3. Learning something new is always fun for me.

**Try It 3**

Decide where each of the sentences below might fit in a paragraph. Write *T* if it could be a *topic sentence*, *D* if it could be a *detail*, and *C* if it could be part of a conclusion. Pay attention to the ideas in the sentence and to the transition words.

_____ 1. To sum it all up, getting the leading role in my first high-school play probably did more for my self-confidence than anything else that happened freshman year.

_____ 2. Have you ever wondered what it is like to be a circus clown?

_____ 3. Finally, the game was over, and all the work of the last few months had paid off.

_____ 4. However, the flowers just weren't growing.

_____ 5. Another case of mumps was reported early that morning.

_____ 6. A storm at sea can be both frightening and exciting, especially if you are in a small boat.

## PRACTICING THE PROCESS

### Gerry's Essay

Gerry broke up his thesis statement into two parts. He used the first part to write the topic sentence for the first paragraph. Now he wants to use the rest of it in his conclusion. He realizes that he must do more than say that there are some things he likes and some things he doesn't. After thinking about it for a while, Gerry decides to contrast pairs of details from his essay to show how he feels.

| POSITIVE | NEGATIVE |
|---|---|
| never cook a meal | never taste a strawberry |
| never get wet in the rain | never hear a live concert |
| never drive in traffic jams | never own your own car |

Gerry decides that the new technology he had imagined may make life a lot easier, but it also may make it more boring. Machines seem to get in the way of life.

This is Gerry's final paragraph. Like the other paragraphs he has written, it is a first draft.

```
Technology will make life easier, but it will also make it more bor-
ing. People will never have to cook a meal, get wet when it rains, or
drive in traffic jams. On the other hand, people will never have a
chance to taste fresh strawberries, hear a live concert, or even
driving their own cars. By taking care of everything for everybody
technology will take away our chance to enjoy life directly.
```

Notice that Gerry didn't use any of the words from his thesis statement, but he did use the ideas.

---

### Your Essay WP

Think about your essay so far. Can you make a statement that sums up what you think is most important about what you have written? Also, think about your readers. What do you want them to think or feel?

On the paper on which you have started your essay, write the conclusion of your essay, giving yourself and your reader an idea that sums up what you have been writing about. Look back at your thesis statement to see how you felt about your topic when you began. Now that you have written at length about the topic, you might find that your ideas have changed. ***It is all right if your ideas change. In fact, it is a sign that you are really thinking while you write.*** Use the final paragraph to add ideas or to sum up what you have already said. Don't worry about all the words and spellings at this time. You will have plenty of chances later on to make changes. Remember to save your paper.

---

***THINK ABOUT*** Gerry's last paragraph. What changes do you think he might want to make when he starts to revise his essay?

# *REVISING*

Some revising can be done as a completely separate step from writing, but some revising cannot be separated from writing (especially if you use a word processor). In these lessons, you will watch another student go through the process of revising an essay. Then you will take your own essay through each of these stages of revision:

- Breaking things up.

- Adding things.

- Taking things out.

- Combining things.

- Replacing things.

Each stage will give you an opportunity to think about what you have written, decide whether you have said things exactly the way you wanted to, and make whatever changes you think are needed.

# Breaking Things Up

*Break up a long paragraph if it develops two main ideas.*

**WARMUP**

When you look at a first draft, see if it is balanced. All the paragraphs in a good school essay should be about the same in length. This shows that each idea has been developed with enough details to make it interesting. You don't even have to read the draft to look for this balance.

**Try It 1**

Which of these drafts has balanced paragraphs?

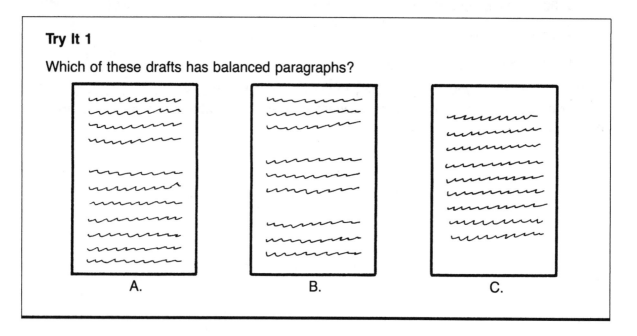

A.                     B.                     C.

In the exercise you just did, Draft B was balanced. Draft C had a paragraph that looked as if it was made up of one sentence. Draft A had one very long paragraph. When you spot a very long paragraph, read it carefully. It may have more than one main idea. Here is a long paragraph from Jessie's first draft of her essay about trying out for the track team.

Our high school turned out one of the best track teams in the state. As a result, a lot of freshmen showed up for the trials, and not everyone made it. I had been a good runner in junior high school, winning the half-mile race in the town-wide Sports Day. However, I wasn't the only good runner in town. There was going to be stiff competition from at least twenty other freshmen who wanted to be part of the Rams. I had to do the best job I had ever done in my life. The day of the tryouts I woke up early, did some stretches, and had some fruit, toast, and yogurt. After breakfast, I sat quietly for a while. My junior high coach had taught me to close my eyes and think about what I wanted the day to be like. In my head I could hear the starter's voice yelling ''Ready, Set, Go.'' I leaped into the race, felt the wind whistle by me, and raced across the finish line-- first. After fifteen minutes I stopped thinking about what was going to happen and left the house to make it happen.

In her long paragraph Jessie had really developed two main ideas. The first idea was about the competition she was going to face at the trials. The second idea was about her preparation for the trials. When she read her draft over, Jessie realized that it should be broken into two parts. She used the paragraph symbol [¶] to remind her to break this long section up when she wrote the final version. This is what her paper looked like when she made this addition. Notice that she put it in pencil both in the body of the text and in the margin, so that she wouldn't forget what she had to do.

. . . I had to do the best job I had ever done in my life. The day of the  /new ¶

tryouts I woke up early. . . .

---

**Try It 2**

Read this paragraph from the middle part of Elena's essay about her summer job as a volunteer in an animal shelter. It is the longest paragraph in her essay, and Elena thinks it might make two paragraphs.

[1] The first person in to work every morning was responsible for checking the water bowls. [2] Every cat and dog had its own bowl and, depending on how many animals there were in the shelter, that meant filling anywhere from twenty to thirty bowls with fresh water. [3] Although that sounds like a lot of work, I didn't really mind it, so I usually tried to be the first person in. [4] The animals were so eager for human company that they tried to lick your hand as you filled the water bottle that fit on the top of each cage. [5] I spent a little time with each cat or dog and a lot of time with each puppy or kitten. [6] The reward for getting in early to water the animals was that you didn't have to clean the cages. [7] Every volunteer knew that the morning cleanup was the worst job in the place. [8] It was messy, hot, and smelly. [9] The cages were built with wire mesh bottoms that fit over a pan lined with newspaper. [10] The cleaner took out the pan, emptied it, lined it with fresh newspaper and put the pan back under the cage. [11] The cats, of course, had a pan of kitty litter to scratch in and that had to be changed too. [12] When the cleanup job was finished, it was feeding time.

1. Which sentences develop the first idea? _____
2. Which sentence begins the second main idea? _____
3. Which sentences develop the second idea? _____
4. Between which two sentences should Elena put the symbol (¶), which shows where the long paragraph should be broken up? _____

# PRACTICING THE PROCESS

## Gerry's Essay

The first thing that Gerry notices when he looks at his first draft is that the second paragraph is very long. He reads it to see how many main ideas there are and realizes that there are two—one about transportation and one about what kind of job he has. He knows that he has to break the long paragraph into two shorter ones so that each paragraph will focus on one main idea. He puts the paragraph symbol (¶) before the sentence that will begin the new paragraph.

> Getting to work is very easy. No one needs a car. Right outside the door is a moving walkway that takes me to a soler-powered transporter. Lots of things in the year 2000 use solar energy. Even my food is cooked by the sun. Anyway, it travels through the tubes that connect all the buildings in this area and stops right at at my office. ¶ I have   /new ¶
> the same job as everyone else I know. I feed information into a huge computer that runs the city. Nobody likes this work but there are no other jobs anymore. Fortunately, though, we only have to work for four hours a day, and then we can do what we want.

When he writes the final copy, he will make this into two paragraphs.

What other changes do you think Gerry may want to make?

---

### Your Essay [WP]

Look at the draft of your essay. If one section is longer than the others, decide if that section discusses one main idea or two. Ask yourself these questions:

> What is the main idea of my paragraph?
> What sentences develop that topic?
> Do some sentences develop another idea?

If you find that you have developed more than one idea in the long section, break it up into two parts. Insert a paragraph symbol [¶] between the sentence that will be the last sentence of one paragraph and the first sentence of the other. Then make a note in the margin so that you won't forget to make this change when you write the final copy.

Make sure that the long paragraph contains two main ideas before you make it into two paragraphs. Sometimes a paragraph runs long because you have put in details that should not be there. The next lesson will show you how to revise for sentences that do not belong.

Save your essay.

# *Taking Things Out*

*Take out words and sentences that do not focus on the main idea of the paragraph.*
*Take out ideas and words that are repeated unnecessarily.*

## WARMUP

Have you ever asked a six-year-old what kind of day it has been? If so, you know the answer goes something like this:

> *Well, we went to the beach. I like the beach especially when my Dad takes us. He always buys us ice cream because he says that's what you need to cool you off. This room is cool. That's because it has an air conditioner. An air conditioner makes you cool. So does a fan. My bedroom is cool when I have the air conditioner on. But my Mom says it makes too much noise. She doesn't like noise. She calls lots of things noise. Like the music my sister plays.*

There is no possibility of paragraph structure in this kind of speech or thought because there is no main idea. Instead there are a series of thoughts connected by association. Talking about getting cool from eating ice cream leads to the thought that the room is cool, which leads to the thought that machines can make you cool. The comment that the air conditioner makes noise leads to the thought that Mom doesn't like noise, and so on. This kind of speech can go on forever, unless someone stops it.

Writers, no matter how old they are, sometimes stray from the main idea of the paragraph they are writing. This can happen when a word in the sentence they are writing makes another idea come immediately to mind. If the new idea is not connected to the main idea of the paragraph, the writer is said to have **digressed**—or strayed—from the topic. A sentence that strays from the main idea is called a **digression**.

---

### Try It

Read each paragraph and cross out the sentence that doesn't belong. Circle the word or words in the preceding sentence that probably caused the digression.

1. Why do exam writers always ask you to write about the best thing that ever happened to you or the worst job you ever had? They seem to have forgotten that most lives are filled with things that aren't so bad, days that are pretty good, and jobs that are so-so. Why don't they ever ask us to write about the ordinary things that happen every day? It would be a snap to write a couple of paragraphs about sleeping through the alarm clock. That happened to me yesterday and it really made the rest of the day awful. Then the essay could describe how you decide what cereal to have for breakfast and what color shirt you want to wear. Such a topic would produce five paragraphs filled with details, realism, and dullness.

---

continued . . .

2. We get so many different kinds of catalogs in our house, we could start a catalog library. We get catalogs for baby clothes, expensive garden tools, expensive vacations. The fact that I am the youngest person in our house, that we live in an apartment, and that we visit grandma every year for our vacation doesn't seem to bother the catalog people at all. Although one year, right after Mom went back to work, we took a vacation to Canada. Well, anyway, even though we don't buy anything by mail, I still like to look at all the things that are available. I guess it is really a kind of window shopping without windows—and without stores.

## PRACTICING THE PROCESS

### Gerry's Essay

While he was reading the long second paragraph, Gerry noticed two sentences that strayed from the main idea. He drew a line through them to show that he would take them out of his final draft. Then he read the paragraph to himself without these two sentences. He realized that the word *anyway*, which is the first word in the sentence that follows the digression, was no longer necessary. He took that out too.

Getting to work is very easy. No one needs a car. Right outside the
door is a moving walkway that takes me to a soler-powered tran-
porter. ~~Lots of things in the year 2000 use solar energy. Even my~~
~~food is cooked by the sun.~~ ~~Anyway,~~ It travels through the tubes that
connect all the buildings in this area and stops right at at my
office.

Gerry reads the rest of the draft to check for digressions or other unnecessary words and phrases. In the paragraph that describes what he does after work, he finds that he has said the same thing twice. In this case, he feels that repeating the idea doesn't add to the paragraph, so he draws a pencil line through the sentence to show that he intends to take it out.

. . . Sometimes, though, what I like best is just to go home and
spend the evening reading. ~~Sometimes an evening of reading is what I~~
~~prefer to do.~~ I don't turn on any machines. I just read from a real
book, not a computer.

Gerry has eliminated a digression and a repeated idea. When he looks at the digression again, he decides that the word anyway was a signal that he was getting back to the main idea of the paragraph. Next time, he thought, he would recognize this signal and would check his paragraph immediately.

What other changes do you think Gerry may want to make?

74

**Your Essay** [WP]

Look at the draft of your essay. Think about the main idea of each paragraph. Read each sentence to make sure that it belongs. Are there any signal words like *anyway* that might indicate you have made a digression? If you find a sentence that doesn't belong, cross it out. Read the paragraph again, without the digression. Does it read smoothly? Should you add something or take something out?

Now check your draft for words or ideas that are repeated unnecessarily. Cross out words and sentences you do not need anymore. Make sure you have marked your paper clearly and accurately, so that you will understand the changes when it is time to copy your paper over.

Save your essay.

# *Adding Things*

*Add specific details to make descriptions more complete.*

## WARMUP

What does the following sentence tell you about the experiment?

> It was a dangerous experiment.

Does the sentence below give you any more information than the first one?

> It was a risky experiment.

Suppose that instead of substituting a synonym for **dangerous**, you added details to **It was a dangerous experiment**. What would sentences like the ones below tell you about the experiment?

> The fumes were poisonous.
> I had to heat the chemicals over a flame.
> The chemicals I was mixing could explode.
> If I touched the mixture, I could burn myself.

You have learned how to improve sentences by substituting more interesting and specific words for general words such as **nice** and **good**:

> **It was a nice day.**
> It was a beautiful day.
> It was a thrilling day.

> **The movie was good.**
> The movie was enjoyable.
> The movie was stupendous.

Substituting another word, however, does not always make the description more complete. There is another way to make descriptions like **It was a nice day** and **The movie was good** less vague and general. You can add sentences that illustrate very specifically what you understand "nice" and "good" to mean:

> **It was a nice day.**
> The sun was shining.
> The flowers were in bloom.
> There was no school.
> I had no homework to do.

> **The movie was good.**
> The story was exciting.
> The screenplay was well written.
> The director kept the action going.
> The actors were convincing.
> It was well photographed.

The details in the additional sentences are not substitutes or synonyms. Instead, they expand the meaning of the first sentence. They tell exactly what made the day nice or what made the movie good.

---

**Try It 1**

Put a check mark in the blank next to each sentence that expands, or adds something new to the meaning of the first sentence in the group.

*Example:* Her room is not very neat.

  ✓  a. There are clothes all over the floor.

  ✓  b. Dirty plates are under the bed.

      c. Her room is very messy looking.

  ✓  d. A wet towel is hanging on the chair.

1. This is an excellent paper.

      a. The main idea is clearly stated.

      b. It is a very good paper.

      c. There are good supporting details.

      d. The conclusion is strong.

      e. This paper is above average.

2. It was a difficult job.

      a. It was a very hard job.

      b. The basement was filthy.

      c. All the cartons were heavy.

      d. The job was not easy to do.

      e. Everything had to be carried up a steep flight of stairs.

3. Danita is a good worker.

      a. She is always on time.

      b. She never makes mistakes.

      c. She is a fine worker.

      d. She is very careful.

      e. She finishes things quickly.

**Try It 2**

Write three sentences that add new details to each of the sentences below.

*Example:*  Josh did well on the test.

*He understood all the questions.*

*He knew all the answers.*

*He had time to finish everything.*

1. We had a good meal.

_____

_____

_____

2. Our vacation was a lot of fun.

_____

_____

_____

## PRACTICING THE PROCESS

### Gerry's Essay

Gerry has spent some time taking out sentences that do not belong in his essay. Now he has started to think about words and sentences he needs to add. As he rereads the first paragraph, he decides that he needs some transitions. Notice that he adds the word *instead* to connect the third and fourth sentences. He also adds at the same time to connect the next-to-last and last sentences. After he has made this change, he realizes that he also needs a transition between the first and second paragraphs, so he adds a new final sentence to the first paragraph.

Because of the changes in technology, a typical day in the year 2000 will be very different from what it is now. For one thing, the mornings begin in a different way. There are'nt any alarm clocks anymore. *Instead, a* special device wakes me up. It shakes me out of bed and shakes me onto the floor. The closet door opens automatically, and the exercise equipment comes out. *At the same time,* The Robot-Cook begins heating the food pellets for breakfast. *I am almost ready to leave for work.*

When Gerry gets to the end of the second paragraph, he stops again. He does not think he needs a transition here, but he does want to add a detail about the office. As he makes the change, he is careful to keep a transition to the next paragraph.

Getting to work is very easy. No one needs a car. Right outside the door is a moving walkway that takes me to a soler-powered transporter. ~~Lots of things in the year 2000 use solar energy. Even my food is cooked by the sun. Anyway,~~ It travels through the tubes that connect all the buildings in this area and stops right at at my office.

*I open the door and step into a soundproof room filled with computer terminals.*

What other changes do you think Gerry may want to make?

---

**Your Essay** WP

Read your essay again. Look for places where you want to add more details to expand a description. Look, too, for places where you need words or sentences to connect ideas.

Make your changes on your first draft. Cross out words you do not need anymore. Write new words above the line or in the margin, with an arrow to show where they are to be inserted. Circle sentences and sentence parts that you want to move, and use arrows to show where they are to go. Make sure you have marked your paper clearly and accurately, so that you will understand the changes when it is time to copy your paper over.

Save your essay.

# REVISING 4:

# *Putting Things Together*

*Use relative clauses to combine sentences.*

## WARMUP

There is more than one way to combine the two sentences below. How have they been combined in example A? How have they been combined in example B? What is the difference between the two examples?

**My sister Leona is someone you've met before. She is walking toward us.**

> A. My sister Leona, who is walking toward us, is someone you've met before.
> B. My sister Leona, who is someone you've met before, is walking toward us.

In example A, the most important idea is **My sister Leona is someone you've met before**. The fact that she is walking toward us is less important. In example B, the most important idea is **My sister Leona is walking toward us**. The fact that she is someone you've met before is less important. In each case, the less important idea is inserted into the more important one.

Often when you are writing, you start out with one piece of information about someone or something. You write a sentence. Then you think of another detail about the person or thing you have just described, so you add another sentence:

> The girl turned out to be Leona. She was walking toward us.

Sometimes, for emphasis, you want the two sentences to remain separate. Sometimes, though, your writing is smoother or your meaning is clearer if you combine them in one of these ways:

> The girl who was walking toward us turned out to be Leona.

> The girl, who turned out to be Leona, was walking toward us.

Remember that only you know what you intended to say and what you wanted your readers to think and feel. Before you combine sentences in your own writing, ask yourself these questions:

> Was the second sentence an afterthought, or did I separate these sentences intentionally? Would the second sentence be better as part of the first sentence, or do I want to insert the first sentence into the second one?

When you combine sentences as in the examples above, the group of words that you move from one sentence into another is called a **relative clause**. A relative clause is easy to recognize. It usually begins with **who**, **whom**, **which** or **that**, and it has a verb in it. It is almost like a sentence within a sentence.

Some relative clauses do a special job in a sentence. They answer the question "Which one?" Look at these examples:

The job **which I have in mind** does not pay well. [WHICH JOB?]
The child **whom you remember** is now six feet tall. [WHICH CHILD?]

Without clauses like the ones underlined above, the sentences would not be the same. These relative clauses are **essential**. They add information that is necessary to the meaning of the sentence.

When something else in the sentence already tells **which one**, the relative clause is no longer absolutely necessary. It adds information that is interesting but not essential. Notice what happens in these sentences when the question "Which one?" is answered by the underlined words.

**Alvin's** job, which is difficult and dangerous, does not pay well.
**This huge** person, whom you knew as a child, is my little brother.

Commas separate a relative clause from the rest of the sentence when the relative clause adds information that is not essential to the meaning of the sentence.

Unfortunately, you cannot always tell just from looking at a sentence whether the relative clause in it contains essential information. You have to know ahead of time what meaning is intended. For example, read this sentence:

The birds which began to make annoying sounds at 5 a.m. woke me up.

Does this sentence mean that all of the birds began to make annoying sounds at 5 a.m. and they woke me up? If so, it should be written like this:

The birds, which began to make annoying sounds at 5 a.m., woke me up.

What if the sentence means that only **some** birds woke me up—the birds that began to make annoying sounds at 5 a.m.? In this case, it should be written without commas. The meaning of the sentence would not be the same without the relative clause to tell **which** birds.

If you are the writer of this sentence, only you know which meaning you intended. You have to let your readers know by putting commas in or taking them out.

There is one case, though, in which you never use commas around a relative clause—when the relative clause begins with **that**:

The birds that began to make annoying sounds at 5 a.m. woke me up.
The girl that was walking toward us turned out to be Leona.

The word **that** is a signal that the relative clause is being used to define or tell **which one** and should not be separated by commas. If you are not sure whether to use commas, a good way to test the meaning of your sentence is to try using **that** in the relative clause. If **that** sounds right, then the relative clause adds essential information. Whether you end up using **that** in it, or **who**, **whom**, or **which**, you do not need commas around the relative clause.

## Try It 1

Decide whether the relative clause in each sentence adds essential information. If it does, cross out *which*, *who* or *whom* and write *that* above it. If the relative clause does not add essential information, insert a comma before and after it.

**Example:**    Where is the jacket ~~which~~ *that* Sam borrowed last week?

Miranda's shoes, which are size 12, do not fit anyone else.

1. LuAnn read the story which was the first-place winner in the contest.
2. The man whom you wanted to hire has taken a different job.
3. Great-Uncle Luther's recipe for chicken which I wrote down uses cayenne pepper and walnuts.
4. Customers who expect special treatment are always disappointed.
5. My friend Sandra who is in my English class waited for the 104 bus with me.
6. Roger's system which he claims is foolproof is impossible to learn.
7. The poster which he bought for Nicole cost $10.
8. The *Daily News* which is delivered before breakfast is the only newspaper Si reads.
9. The runner who came in last received a special award.
10. Irene whom you recognized right away has not changed at all.

## Try It 2

Combine each pair of sentences below by making the second one into a relative clause. Use *that*, *which*, or *who* to begin it. Put commas around the relative clause if you think they are needed.

**Example:**    The alarm clock rang at 6 a.m. 6 a.m. is the time I usually get up.

_The alarm clock rang at 6 a.m., which is the time_

_I usually get up._

1. Sonya rushed home to watch *At the World's Edge*. It is her favorite show.

_____

_____

2. Today's episode featured Tory Danger. He is the show's hero.

_____

_____

3. A mysterious woman arrived in Centerville. Tory seemed to know her.

_____

_____

continued . . .

4. The woman was extremely glamorous. She wore dark glasses and high-heeled boots.

_____

_____

5. A letter arrived for Tory. It was postmarked "Shanghai."

_____

_____

6. Tory invited the woman to dinner at Club Eight. It is the most expensive restaurant in town.

_____

_____

7. Dolly Harper saw them going into the restaurant. She is Tory's regular girlfriend.

_____

_____

8. She also saw the letter. Tory accidentally dropped the letter on the street.

_____

_____

9. Sonya wondered whether there was a connection between Shanghai and the mystery woman. Sonya had not moved for an hour.

_____

_____

10. The next episode might answer this question. It would not be on until Monday.

_____

_____

## Try It 3

There is an extra step you can take with some relative clauses. After you have combined sentences, you may find that you can take out part of the relative clause without changing the meaning of the sentence.

The alarm clock rang at 6 a.m., **which is** the time I usually get up.
The alarm clock rang at 6 a.m., the time I usually get up.

continued . . .

Experienced writers often take this additional step in order to make their sentences even smoother. Try it on some other sentences from the last activity.

1. Sonya rushed home to watch *At the World's Edge*, which is her favorite show.

_____

_____

2. Today's episode featured Tory Danger, who is the show's hero.

_____

_____

3. A letter that was postmarked "Shanghai" arrived for Tory.

_____

_____

4. Tory invited the woman to dinner at Club Eight, which is the most expensive restaurant in town.

_____

_____

5. Dolly Harper, who is Tory's regular girlfriend, saw them going into the restaurant.

_____

_____

## PRACTICING THE PROCESS

### Gerry's Essay

Gerry has now made a number of changes in his essay—adding things, taking things out, and even creating a new paragraph. This time, as he looks through what he has written, he sees three pairs of sentences that he thinks would sound better if they were combined. One pair is in the first paragraph, and two are in the fourth paragraph:

Because of the changes in technology, a typical day in the year 2000 will be very different from what it is now. For one thing, the mornings begin in a different way. There are'nt any alarm clocks anymore. *Instead, a* special device wakes me up, ~~It shakes me~~ *by shaking me* out of bed and ~~shakes me~~ onto the floor. The closet door opens automatically, and the exercise equipmnet comes out. *At the same time t*The Robot–Cook begins heating the food pellets for breakfast. *I am almost ready to leave for work.*

Some nights we ride the monorail around the mall to look at the life-like robots, ~~They~~ *that* demonstrate the sports equipment. On weekends we go to Synthesizer concerts. There aren't any live musicians, but we see 3-D videos, *while w*~~We~~ listen to the music, ~~too~~. Sometimes, though, what I like best is just to go home and spend the evening reading. ~~Some- times an evening of reading is what I prefer to do.~~ I don't turn on any machines. I just read from a real book, not a computer.

In paragraph 1, Gerry decides to combine several ideas by changing the structure of the second sentence in the pair and taking out some repeated words. In paragraph 4, he decides to change the first two sentences into one sentence with a relative clause. Then he sees two sentences that are connected by a time relationship. He decides to show that relationship more clearly by combining them with the word *while*.

Notice that Gerry did not combine every group of short sentences or every pair of sentences with related ideas. He did not, for example, combine the first two sentences in the second paragraph:

Getting to work is easy. No one needs a car.

Gerry liked the way these sentences sounded. He only combined sentences that he thought would be smoother or easier to understand if they were rewritten as one sentence.

What other changes do you think Gerry may want to make?

---

**Your Essay** WP

Read your essay again. This time, look for sentences that could be improved by combining them. Remember that there are a number of ways of combining. You saw some of them in Gerry's essay. Think carefully before you combine sentences. Ask yourself these questions:

- Which way do they sound better—separate or combined?
- Which way do make the point more clearly—separate or combined?
- When I combine, which idea do I want to emphasize?

Make your changes on your first draft. Cross out words you do not need anymore. Write new words above the line or in the margin, with an arrow to show where they are to be inserted. Circle sentences and sentence parts that you want to move, and use arrows to show where they are to go. Make sure you have marked your paper clearly and accurately, so that you will understand the changes when it is time to copy your paper over.

Save your essay.

# Replacing Things

*A strong opening and closing make your writing more interesting.*

## WARMUP

Which opening sentences make you want to read the rest of the essay?

1. Rae Murray's specialty is painting very realistic pictures of flowers.
2. Rae Murray's flowers look so real, people are sometimes tempted to water them.
3. Did you ever try to hold a cat that was hissing and clawing?
4. It was extremely difficult to learn to control my temper.

A good opening is one of the most important parts of your essay. It gets your readers involved in what you think and feel and makes them want to go on reading. Sometimes a topic sentence makes an interesting opening. Sometimes, however, you want to replace the topic sentence with a sentence that does not necessarily express the main idea but does hook your readers. In sentences 2 and 3 above, the use of specific words instead of general ones and the introduction of dramatic or humorous examples help draw the readers in.

---

### Try It 1

Here are four ways to make an opening sentence lively enough so that the reader will want to know what comes next.

| | |
|---|---|
| 1. ASK A QUESTION | Could you stay calm with your worst enemy just inches from your nose? |
| 2. ADD MORE SPECIFIC DETAILS | From the time I could walk, my temper got me in trouble every day of my life. |
| 3. BE DRAMATIC OR HUMOROUS | No one can imagine what it is like to have a temper that can be set off as easily as a firecracker on the Fourth of July. |
| 4. SHOW INSTEAD OF TELL | "Hey, Freckle Juice," was all I needed to hear before my fists were doubled up and I was ready to start swinging. |

Rewrite the sentence below in each of these four ways.

The moment in my life I would like to relive is the time that I was in the first-grade play.

1. _____

_____

2. _____

_____

---

continued...

3. _____

_____

4. _____

_____

Closings are almost as important as openings. You want to introduce your subject with a blast of trumpets, and you want to conclude with cheering and applause. Instead, you often sum up what you have said with concluding sentences like these:

1. That is why I never spoke to her again.
2. As I have pointed out, this is an important book for many reasons.
3. Now you know why I don't like spiders.

The feeling your audience is left with at the end of your essay depends a great deal on what you say in your concluding paragraph. Even without reading the whole essay, you will feel something when you read final sentences that use techniques like these.

RESTATING THE MAIN IDEA

I knew that from that moment on, my life would be completely different.

ASKING A QUESTION

At what point do we stop to think, "Will there be enough time to save these animals?"

ADDING A PERSONAL OPINION

When the long, long day of spring cleanup was finally over, I came to the conclusion that neatness is a virtue I may someday develop but I will never love.

---

**Try It 2**

The following sentences are boring. Rewrite them to make them more interesting. Restate the idea, ask a question, or add a personal opinion. First, read the example.

*Example:* That is what happened the first time I asked someone to the movies.
*If I don't want to go to the movies alone the rest of my life, I think I'd better learn how to ask for a date.*

1. The game was over and I went home.

_____

_____

---

continued . . .

2. So that was what happened to the duck I trained. _____

_____

3. At the end of two weeks, I finished my course in rock climbing.

_____

_____

4. After what happened, I didn't want to try out for the drama club again.

_____

_____

5. That is the reason the valve on my trumpet got stuck.

_____

_____

## PRACTICING THE PROCESS

### Gerry's Essay

Gerry reads the opening and closing paragraphs again to see how he can make them more interesting. He likes the last sentence of the essay a lot and decides to keep it just the way it is, but he wants to introduce the idea the sentence expresses at the beginning of the paragraph. He thinks for a while, doodles on the paper, writes some words, erases them, then adds a sentence in pencil above the line. He reads further and changes the general word **boring** to the more specific word **artificial**. Finally, he corrects the ending of the second last sentence to make it parallel.

*It will be hard to get away from machines in the year 2000.*
Technology will make life easier, but it will also make life more
*artificial*
~~boring~~. People will never have to cook a meal, get wet when it rains,
*traffic*
or drive in ~~trafic~~ jams. On the other hand, people will never have a
chance to taste fresh strawberries, hear a live concert, or even
*drive*
~~driving~~ their own cars. By taking care of everything for everybody,
technology will take away our chance to enjoy life directly.

He is still not completely satisfied with the first paragraph. When he reads the draft to see what other changes he can make, he replaces the general phrase **comes out** with the more specific phrase **rolls out**. The opening still bothers him. He knows that asking a question is one way to begin, but the question he comes up with doesn't seem to add anything. He wants to be dramatic, and he wants to emphasize how technology has come to control and change the way we live. He thinks for a few minutes, then crosses out the first revision and replaces it with a sentence that is much more dramatic.

In the year 2000 technology will dominate our lives so that even everyday events are almost unrecognizable. What will a typical day in the year 2000 be like? ~~Because of the changes in technology, a typical day in the year 2000 will be very different from what it is now~~. For one thing, the mornings begin in a different way. There ~~are'nt~~ aren't any alarm clocks anymore. Instead, a ~~A~~ special device wakes me up, ~~It shakes~~ by shaking me out of bed and onto the floor. The closet door opens automatically, and the exercise equipment rolls ~~equipmnct comes~~ out. At the same time, the ~~The~~ Robot-Cook begins heating the food pellets for breakfast.

---

**Your Essay** WP

Read your opening and closing paragraphs. Do they say what you want them to say? Do they say it in a way that is interesting or dramatic? Imagine that you are the reader for whom this essay was written. What would be a good way to capture your attention?

Look, too, for any other changes that you think would improve your essay. Do you want to substitute more interesting or specific words for words that are too general? Do you have any errors in parallelism that need to be corrected? Is there anything else you want to add or take out?

Make all the changes you want to make. Then put your paper aside and do not think about it for a day or two. When you read it over before making your final copy, you will then be able to enjoy what you have written.

# *EDITING*

Editing is the final step in the writing process. At this stage, you concentrate on making your manuscript look good so that it will be easy to read. You learn some tricks to make proofreading easier. The Editing Handbook helps you check and correct your spelling, punctuation, and usage. Then, using the model for manuscript form, you put the title on your paragraph and write the final copy.

# *Editing Handbook*

*Writers follow editing rules to make their writing easier to read.*

This Handbook will help make your writing easier for others to read. When you edit your writing, check it for

- Capitalization
- Punctuation
- Usage
- Spelling

## CAPITALIZATION

When a word begins with a capital letter, the reader knows that it is special.

Read each rule and then apply it by capitalizing the correct word in the Practice Sentence.

1. Capitalize the first word—

   - *in a sentence*

     **A** sunny day always makes me feel good.

     PRACTICE: how does a rainy day make you feel?

   - *in a quotation*

     Marca asked, "**W**hen do we start filming?"

     PRACTICE: Boris answered, "wait until I finish the script."

   - *in the greeting or closing of a letter*

     **D**ear Ms. Ferretti:
     **S**incerely,

     PRACTICE: very truly yours,

2. Capitalize the word *I*.

     "If **I** ask for more, will you give it to me?"

     PRACTICE: "How much do you want?" i asked.

3. Capitalize the *first* word and all the words in a title *except* for short words like *a*, *an*, *at*, *for*, *in*, *of*, *the*, *to*.

     **O**ne **D**ay at a **T**ime
     "**L**ost in the **S**tars"

     PRACTICE: "for once in my life"

4. Capitalize words that name or refer to a particular person, place, thing, or group. Here are some examples:

- ● *Months, days, holidays*

    **A**pril, **T**uesday, **L**abor **D**ay

    PRACTICE:    february    wednesday    christmas

- ● *Businesses, institutions, government departments*

    **M**obil **O**il **C**ompany, **W**indham **H**igh **S**chool,
    **D**epartment of the **A**rmy

    PRACTICE:    ibm    harvard university    state department

- ● *Historical events, documents*

    **R**evolutionary **W**ar, **D**eclaration of **I**ndependence

    PRACTICE:    vietnam war    constitution

- ● *Brand names*

    **M**oonglow flashlights

    PRACTICE:    tasteful fruit cocktail

- ● *Nationalities, languages, geographical names*

    **K**enyan, **S**panish, **S**arasota, **H**udson **R**iver

    PRACTICE:    french    guatemalan    portuguese    lake erie

---

**CAPITALIZATION REVIEW**

Add a capital letter where you need to in each sentence.

1. Do i snore very often?

2. Sandy said, "how soon will dinner be ready?"

3. does the music class meet every day?

4. The first friday of the month is when we practice.

5. Ian is the manager of the flakee pie company.

6. Jan wrote a paper about the civil war.

7. Why don't we ever get a good bread, like soft-chew?

8. We plan to canoe down the allegheny river.

9. in the first chapter you learn about prepositions.

10. Lee wants to visit his cousins in hawaii.

## PUNCTUATION

### End Marks

End marks tell the reader where a sentence ends.

Read each rule and then apply it by adding a period or a question mark in the Practice Sentence.

1. When a sentence makes a statement, make sure it ends with a period.

    The light was left on all night.

    PRACTICE: The electric bill will be high

2. When a sentence asks a question, make sure it ends with a question mark.

    When did Edison invent the phonograph?

    PRACTICE: Did he get a lot of money for it

### Commas

Commas separate words, groups of words, or sentences.

Read each rule and then apply it by adding a comma in the Practice Sentence.

1. When two sentences are combined with a conjunction like **and**, **but**, or **or**, make sure there is a comma before the conjunction.

    The TV broadcaster predicted rain, but the weather was actually very hot and sunny.

    PRACTICE: Some people brought umbrellas to work with them and some people wore heavy raincoats.

2. When a sentence begins with a long group of introductory words, make sure there is a comma after the group of words.

    When the dishes are done, you can do your homework.
    If you want to go to the movies, you must first mow the lawn.
    At the end of the day, Todd had finished all his chores.
    Sitting in his favorite chair, Tom drank a cup of tea and read the paper.

    PRACTICE: When Joyce reads your letter she will be surprised.
    If Sam wanted her to come with us he should have telephoned her.
    In the beginning of the chapter the detective knows who the criminal is.
    Resting with her head on her paws Sylvia's dog waited patiently.

3. When you have a list of three or more things in a sentence, make sure there is a comma between each item.

    The cook needed more eggs, butter, and cheese.
    Jeremy wanted to know who was going, where they were going, and how they were going to get there.

    PRACTICE: Mona likes pepperoni onions and mushrooms on her pizza.
    Karen watched while Kate did the dishes Rosa swept the floor and Nick put away the food.

4. Use commas to separate a nonessential relative clause from the rest of the sentence.

> The new play, which everyone said was so funny, didn't make me laugh once.

> PRACTICE: The audience which seemed to laugh every thirty seconds or so obviously didn't agree with me.

## Apostrophes

Apostrophes have special uses.

Read each rule and then apply it by adding an apostrophe to a word in the Practice.

1. When you write a contraction like *isn't* or *there's*, make sure there is an apostrophe.

| | |
|---|---|
| haven't | there's |
| isn't | where's |
| can't | she's |
| doesn't | you're |
| aren't | I'll |

> PRACTICE: They havent asked.     Theres the package.
>
> It isnt possible.     Wheres the book?
>
> She cant find it.     Hes still waiting.
>
> It doesnt fit.     Youre late.
>
> We arent going.     Ill see you.

2. When you use a possessive noun to show that something belongs to someone, make sure that you write it with an apostrophe.

| | |
|---|---|
| Lee's sweater | boys' sweaters |
| a judge's decision | two judges' decisions |
| a woman's right | women's rights |

> PRACTICE: Borrow Maureens book.
>
> The towns vote went to Mayor Ramsey.
>
> Our library has a childrens hour every day.

---

**PUNCTUATION REVIEW**

Add periods, question marks, commas, and apostrophes where they are needed.

1. Last night's performance which neither of us saw was best.

2. Theres a letter on the hall table for you.

3. Kathy climbed the hill found a sunny spot and sat down to wait for her friend.

4. When the bell rang Lucy closed her book bag.

5. Hes waiting to hear from you before he leaves the house.

---

continued...

6. The author wrote another chapter and the publisher sent her more money.

7. Humming quietly to himself the photographer shot the picture.

8. At the end of the marking period all the work must be made up.

9. They just wont do anything we want them to do.

10. After the dance was over we went to the shore for a cookout.

## USAGE

Ask yourself these questions as you read over your paragraph.

1. Did I use the correct form of each verb?

2. Did I use the correct form of each pronoun?

3. Did I use the correct form of each plural?

## SPELLING

Here is a list of commonly misspelled words. Look at each word. Then close your eyes and try to picture the word as if you were seeing it on a chalkboard. Finally, write the word in the space provided. After you have practiced spelling these words, look at your paragraph and see if you need to make any changes.

1. writing _____
2. arctic _____
3. effect _____
4. personal _____
5. incredible _____
6. embarrass _____
7. accommodate _____
8. privilege _____
9. sincerely _____
10. advice _____
11. certainly _____
12. lose _____
13. criticize _____
14. possible _____
15. receive _____

16. mysterious _____
17. similar _____
18. descendant _____
19. breathe _____
20. occurring _____
21. explanation _____
22. necessary _____
23. occasion _____
24. formerly _____
25. valuable _____
26. description _____
27. opinion _____
28. height _____
29. effect _____
30. probably _____

continued...

31. miniature _____

32. separate _____

33. business _____

34. calendar _____

35. quiet _____

36. especially _____

37. interest _____

38. succeed _____

39. mathematics _____

40. against _____

41. heroes _____

42. rhythm _____

43. except _____

44. adolescent _____

45. magnificent _____

46. through _____

47. pleasant _____

48. belief _____

49. recommend _____

50. guarantee _____

*EDITING 2:*

# *Proofreading*

*Proofreading and editing are the last steps you do before making the final copy.*

## WARMUP

Use these marks when you proofread.

| | |
|---|---|
| Capitalize a word. | _L_<br>/leila |
| Change a capital letter to lower case. | Leila started ⱨigh school this year. |
| Add punctuation. | At the end of this making period‚she will be a sophomore |
| Take out a word. | Leila started high school this ~~this~~ year. |
| Add a word. | Leila started high school ^this^ year. |
| Correct a misspelled word | Leila stareted high s͜c͜ool this year. |

To train yourself to be a good proofreader, do the following:
- Read sentences word by word.
- Read a word you're not sure of letter by letter.
- Write corrections neatly.
- Read and correct a second time.

## PRACTICE

These exercises will help you train your eye so that you can become a better proofreader.

1. Cross out the extra letter.

   agreeeable   completting   excellling   horribble   allowwance

   Have you been invited to Renee'ss party?

2. Cross out the extra word in each sentence.

   The Bay High Blue Birds have not not lost a game yet.

   Did you ever meet the cousin of George's who who has a black belt in karate?

   At at the end of the day, Leslie can hardly wait to get home.

   Barbara borrowed a broom and a a mop to clean up the floor.

3. Cross out the letters that are reversed and write them correctly above the word.

The strom caused widespread damage.

There was a falsh of lightning and a roll of thunder.

No one is allowed to stop wroking until the job is done.

How many birdges are there across this river?

## PRACTICING THE PROCESS

### Gerry's Essay

This is what Gerry's revised essay looked like after he had proofread it.

In the year 2000 technology will dominate our lives so that even everyday events are almost unrecognizable. ~~What will a typical day in the year 2000 be like?~~ e

~~Because of the changes in technology, a typical day in the year 2000 will be very different from what it is now.~~ For one thing, the mornings begin in a different way. There ~~are'nt~~ aren't any alarm clocks anymore. Instead, a A special device wakes me up. ~~It shakes~~ by shaking me out of bed and ~~shakes me~~ onto the floor. The closet door opens automatically, and the exercise ~~equipmnet comes~~ equipment rolls out. At the same time, the ~~The~~ Robot-Cook begins heating the food pellets for breakfast. I am almost ready to leave for work.

Getting to work is very easy. No one needs a car. Right outside the door is a moving walkway that takes me to a ~~soler~~ solar-powered transporter. ~~Lots of things in the year 2000 use solar energy. Even my food is cooked by the sun. Anyway,~~ I It travels through the tubes that connect I open the door and step into a soundproof room filled with computer terminals ¶ all the buildings in this area and stops right ~~at~~ at my office. I have the same job as everyone else I know. I feed information into a huge computer that runs the city. Nobody likes this work, but there are no other kinds of jobs anymore. Fortunately, though, we only have to work for four hours a day, and then we can do what we want.

Some nights we ride the monorail around the mall to look at the ~~liflike~~ lifelike robots that ~~They~~ demonstrate the sports equipment. On weekends we go to synthesizer concerts. There aren't any live musicians, but we see 3-D videos, while we listen to the music, ~~too.~~ Sometimes, though, what I like best is just to go home and spend the evening reading. ~~Sometimes an evening of reading is what I prefer to do.~~ I don't turn on any machines. I just read from a real book, not a computer.

*It will be hard to get away from machines in the year 2000.*
∧ Technology will make life easier, but it will also make life more
*artificial*
∧ ~~boring~~. People will never have to cook a meal, get wet when it rains,
*traffic*
or drive in ∧ ~~trafic~~ jams. On the other hand, people will never have a chance to taste fresh strawberries, hear a live concert, or even
*drive*
∧ ~~driving~~ their own cars. By taking care of everything for everybody ∧ technology will take away our chance to enjoy life directly.

---

**Your Essay** WP

Take out your revised essay. Proofread it by reading it over word by word and—for words you are not sure of—letter by letter. Look for errors in punctuation too. When you think you have caught all the errors, read it again.

# Final Copy

*The final copy always looks good.*

Before making the final copy, Gerry reviewed the rules his teacher had given to the class.

1. Put a heading in the upper right-hand corner of your paper. The heading consists of

   Your name
   Your class
   The date

2. Put the title of the essay on a separate line in the center of the page. Follow the rules for capitalizing titles.

3. Leave a margin top and bottom and left and right.

4. Indent each paragraph five spaces or five letters.

Then he wrote his final copy.

Gerry Giannetti
English 9
February 17, 1989

A Look at the Future

In the year 2000 technology will dominate our lives so that even everyday events are almost unrecognizable. For one thing, the mornings begin in a different way. There aren't any alarm clocks anymore. Instead, a special device wakes me up by shaking me out of bed and onto the floor. The closet door opens automatically, and the exercise equipment rolls out. At the same time, the Robot-Cook begins heating the food pellets for breakfast. I am almost ready to leave for work.

Getting to work is very easy. No one needs a car. Right outside the door is a moving walkway that takes me to a solar-powered transporter. It travels through the tubes that connect all the buildings in this area and stops right at my office. I open the door and step into a soundproof room filled with computer terminals.

I have the same job as everyone else I know. I feed information into a huge computer that runs the city. Nobody likes this work, but there are no other kinds of jobs anymore. Fortunately, though, we only have to work for four hours a day, and then we can do what we want.

Some nights we ride the monorail around the mall to look at the lifelike robots that demonstrate the sports equipment. On weekends we go to synthesizer concerts. There aren't any live musicians, but we see 3-D videos while we listen to the music. Sometimes, though, what I like best is just to go home and spend the evening reading. I don't turn on any machines. I just read from a real book, not a computer.

It will be hard to get away from machines in the year 2000. Technology will make life easier, but it will also make life more artificial. People will never have to cook a meal, get wet when it rains, or drive in traffic jams. On the other hand, people will never have a chance to taste fresh strawberries, hear a live concert, or even drive their own cars. By taking care of everything for everybody, technology will take away our chance to enjoy life directly.

---

**Your Essay** 🖳

On a fresh sheet of paper, write the final copy of your revised and proofread essay.

---

Congratulations!

You have now written an essay that other people can enjoy reading. What you have learned does not stop with this essay. You can apply it to many other kinds of essays. Whatever kind of writing you do, the process will always be the same—prewriting, writing, revising, and editing.

# OTHER KINDS OF ESSAYS

Up till now, you have been working with the personal essay. In a personal essay, you describe how **you** feel about someone or something that you know about. This kind of essay has **you** at the center.

There are two other kinds of essays you are asked to write in school. One is the **expository essay**. In an expository essay, you describe or discuss a topic without directly expressing your own feelings. In expository writing, the **subject** is at the center.

The third kind of essay, the **persuasive essay**, has a special purpose—to get someone to agree with what the writer says and even to do what the writer suggests. When you write a persuasive essay, you begin with an idea that you have a strong opinion about. But along with the information about it, you also give strong, dramatic, and emotional reasons for what you say to persuade your audience to agree with your opinion. You might end the essay by asking your audience to do something. In persuasive writing, the **audience** is at the center.

# Preparing to Write An Expository Essay

*Expository writing shows or explains.*

Writing that presents straightforward information or that explains something is called **expository** writing. Textbooks, newspaper or magazine articles, recipes, even directions on how to put together a bicycle—all these are examples of expository writing, or **exposition**.

Expository writing deals with such things as—
> How to do something.
> How something works.
> What something is like.
> How something happens naturally.
> How something happened in the past.

The following are all possible topics that call for an expository essay:
> How to make pancakes.
> How a copying machine makes copies.
> What the school rules are.
> How baby ducks learn to follow their mother.
> How people traveled in 1852.

In an expository essay, the writer's job is to make a set of instructions, a process, an idea, an event, or a relationship as clear as possible. The writer of an expository essay is almost in the position of a teacher. They both have the same goal—to help the audience understand something.

A form of expository writing that you probably read or use every day is a set of instructions or directions. For example, a magazine article might have a paragraph that contains instructions like these:

> *To make a green salad, begin by washing and drying half a head of lettuce. Then tear the lettuce leaves into bite-size pieces. Next, peel a cucumber and slice it in thin rounds. In addition, wash two stalks of celery, trim off the ends, and chop the stalks coarsely. Finally, wash two scallions, trim the ends, and cut into thin slices. Toss all the ingredients together in a large bowl until they are well mixed.*

A set of directions includes every step that is needed to make or do something. The steps must be in order, and the order must be clear to the reader. The language must also be very precise. For example, the directions above instruct the reader to "tear," "peel," "slice," "chop," and so on. The reader knows exactly what to do at each stage of the process. There is a very simple way to test whether a set of directions is well written: Can the reader complete the task or arrive at the destination by following the directions?

**Practice 1**

On the lines below, write a set of directions that explains one of the following things:

    a. How to make a bed.
    b. How to get to the gym from your classroom.
    c. How to make an egg salad sandwich (or any other simple recipe).

If possible, let someone try to follow your directions. Check whether you included all the necessary steps and whether the steps are in the right order.

_____

_____

_____

_____

_____

_____

_____

_____

_____

_____

_____

_____

_____

_____

An expository essay can also describe what something is like or explain how something works. This sort of expository essay gives reasons or examples to help the reader understand the explanation. For instance, here is a description of how Middleburgh High School is organized. It explains why students never feel lost there. Notice how specific the details are.

Although there are 2,000 students at Middleburgh High School, the school rarely seems that large. The students are divided into four groups of about 500 students each. These groups are called "houses." One house contains the entire freshman class, and it is located in an annex of the school. The other three houses are mixed, with sophomores, juniors, and seniors in each one. House One is on the first floor of the main building, House Two is on the second floor, and House Three is on the third floor. Each house has its own office and its own guidance counselors. Within the house there are also ten homerooms, where students meet at the beginning of the school day. Each house is like a school within a school, so that students never feel lost at Middleburgh.

## Practice 2

On the lines below, write a paragraph that explains how one of the following is organized:

  a. Your school government.
  b. The public library in your town.
  c. A baseball, basketball, or football team (or any other sports team).

Remember to include specific details. If possible, exchange papers with a classmate when you have finished writing. See whether you understand each other's explanations. Are the reasons or examples clear? Have any important details been left out?

_____

_____

_____

_____

_____

_____

_____

_____

_____

_____

_____

OTHER KINDS OF ESSAYS 2:

# Writing An Expository Essay

*An expository essay focuses on the subject, rather than on the writer or on the audience.*

There is often very little difference in content between a personal essay and an expository essay. What is different is the way the content is organized and presented.

Gerry, the author of "A Look at the Future," was given the following topic for an expository essay:

Compare or contrast at least two changes in the way we live that are the result of advances in technology.

When he started to narrow the topic, he realized that it was similar in many ways to what he had written for his personal essay. In that essay, he had described the changes he thought technology would bring in the future. He had also given his own opinion—he liked some of the changes and did not like others.

This time, instead of turning the essay into a story about his own life, he would stand outside the subject and describe the effects of technology objectively. He would also be organizing his essay in a special way, comparing or contrasting the changes in modern life in order to show their similarities or differences.

Here is the expository essay Gerry wrote. His personal essay is on the following page so that you can compare the two. The notes in the margins point out some of the differences between them.

## Technology Changes Our Lives

The ways in which modern technology has changed people's lives vary a great deal. For instance, the electronic revolution has made many things work faster and more accurately. It has created new ways of doing things. It has also changed or eliminated some of the old ways. Contrasting two changes in the way people live shows the differences in the way that technology has affected modern life.

For example, electronics has changed the world of music by creating the synthesizer. The synthesizer has given listeners a whole new range of sounds that can stand on their own or be combined with other instruments. This electronic advance has also changed the lives of music students and composers. One synthesizer makes it possible for a student to hear and experiment with the sounds of a variety of instruments. A composer can work with a synthesizer as though it were an entire band or orchestra. The synthesizer adds a new element to music—making.

The same principles of electronics, on the other hand, have often had a different effect on people's jobs. Computers do get many jobs done in less time than people do, and they make fewer errors. However, this has sometimes meant that computers replace people on the job.

There are some new jobs available that involve working with computers; but people are beginning to find that there are drawbacks to these jobs. Many workers now do nothing but input data. They frequently have to work at a much faster pace than they used to because the computer keeps track of their speed and the length of time they work. They have little or no contact with other people, and there is no variety in their work. While making some tasks easier, technology has limited these workers' lives.

Technology is capable both of adding to people's lives and of taking something away. The synthesizer has expanded the ways there are of making music. It has given musicians a new tool and audiences a new experience. By contrast, the computer has sometimes taken away people's jobs or changed the nature of their work in a way that they do not like.

# A Look at the Future

In the year 2000 technology will dominate our lives so that even everyday events are almost unrecognizable. For one thing, the mornings begin in a different way. There aren't any alarm clocks anymore. Instead, a special device wakes me up by shaking me out of bed and onto the floor. The closet door opens automatically, and the exercise equipment rolls out. At the same time, the Robot-Cook begins heating the food pellets for breakfast. I am almost ready to leave for work.

Getting to work is very easy. No one needs a car. Right outside the door is a moving walkway that takes me to a solar-powered transporter. It travels through the tubes that connect all the buildings in this area and stops right at my office. I open the door and step into a soundproof room filled with computer terminals.

I have the same job as everyone else I know. I feed information into a huge computer that runs the city. Nobody likes this work, but there are no other kinds of jobs anymore. Fortunately, though, we only have to work for four hours a day, and then we can do what we want.

Some nights we ride the monorail around the mall to look at the lifelike robots that demonstrate the sports equipment. On weekends we go to synthesizer concerts. There aren't any live musicians, but we see 3-D videos while we listen to the music. Sometimes, though, what I like best is just to go home and spend the evening reading. I don't turn on any machines. I just read from a real book, not a computer.

It will be hard to get away from machines in the year 2000. Technology will make life easier, but it will also make life more artificial. People will never have to cook a meal, get wet when it rains, or drive in traffic jams. On the other hand, people will never have a chance to taste fresh strawberries, hear a live concert, or even drive their own cars. By taking care of everything for everybody, technology will take away our chance to enjoy life directly.

## Your Essay WP

On a separate sheet of paper, write an expository essay on the following topic:

Compare or contrast life in two different periods of time.

Use Gerry's expository essay as a model. Remember that when you **compare**, you are exploring the similarities between two or more things. When you **contrast**, you are exploring the differences.

Follow these steps to write your essay:

1. **Narrow the topic.** Choose two time periods that you are interested in and know something about. You might want to use the present and the time when your parents were teenagers, or you might want to go farther back in history than that. Decide whether you want to compare or contrast the two periods of time. Then focus on one or two aspects of those time periods that make the similarities or differences between them stand out. For example, you might want to describe transportation and communication, home life (laundry, food preparation, heating, light, and so on), or social customs.

2. **Brainstorm.** Use the prewriting stage to brainstorm lists of examples and details.

3. **Write a first draft.** Your first draft should include at least four paragraphs. Write an introductory paragraph, at least two paragraphs of comparison or contrast, and a concluding paragraph.

   Describe first one period of time and then the other. Point out the ways in which they are alike or different. Here are some transition and focusing words that can help you:

   | | |
   |---|---|
   | however | though |
   | even though | although |
   | on the other hand | yet |
   | nevertheless | conversely |
   | as opposed to | rather than |
   | in spite of | compared to |
   | similarly | in the same way |
   | as well as | likewise |

4. **Remember that your writing should be objective.** Write from the third-person point of view. Do not give your own opinion or use the pronoun *I*. Your job is just to explain as completely as possible the similarities or differences in the two time periods you have chosen.

5. **Revise your essay.** Do you want to improve the opening or the closing? Do you need to add any details? Do you need to take out anything that does not belong? Do you need to add transitions? Are there any words that need changing? Do you want to combine any ideas?

6. **Edit and proofread your essay.** Then make a clean copy.

# *Preparing to Write a Persuasive Essay*

*Knowing the difference between a fact and an opinion and using sound reasoning are important when you write a persuasive essay.*

When you read an editorial in a newspaper or a speech by a politician, you know that the writer has only one main purpose—to get you to agree with the ideas in the editorial or in the speech. Sometimes you are asked to do something after you have agreed with the ideas. The newspaper editor might suggest that you support a cause; the politician might ask for your vote. Editorials and speeches are used to persuade their readers. Both kinds of writing are forms of the **persuasive essay**.

The persuasive essay, like the other essays you have practiced writing, has a **thesis statement**. In the case of the persuasive essay, the thesis statement lets the reader know the writer's opinion about a particular subject. The thesis statement is then supported with details, the facts that demonstrate the truth of the thesis statement.

A good persuasive essay also points out the other side of the issue. This helps persuade the reader that the writer has a strong case. It says, in effect "Here are some of the things you disagree with about my statement. Let's look at them together."

Here is an example of an editorial in a school newspaper that uses all these techniques. Notice that the writer uses the first person plural form **"we."** This is known as the **editorial "we."**

*Our students need less homework, not more. Before you cancel your subscription to the New Ark High School Gazette, let's make sure that you understand what we mean. By homework we mean the kind of busy work that students either don't do or won't do. We mean the math papers that require parents to take adult education courses at the high school in order to be able to read them. We mean the long-range research papers on subjects that no one is interested in—the ones that end up as rewritten encyclopedia articles.*

*But how will students learn, you may ask? Isn't it necessary to reinforce what they've learned in school so that they'll remember it for more than five minutes? Up till now, we would have gone along with the old notions of homework. Last week, however, we read a report from the Millville school district. They abolished homework as such last year. The school day has been extended to provide for "Preparation Time." Each class period has time built in so that students can prepare for tomorrow's classes. The only thing they do at home is extra reading and computer work. This year, Millville School is the top district in the state. We say, "Let's try it."*

To convince your reader that your idea is worth considering, you must state your thesis so that everyone knows what you are talking about, then give facts to support your opinion. Of course, in order to do this, you must know the difference between a fact and an opinion.

A fact is something that makes you say, "Well, no one can argue with that." A fact is something you can **verify**—that is, you can make sure that it is true. You can look up a fact in a book, or you can experience it yourself. Here are two examples.

Lincoln was shot in 1865.
It is raining.

You can find the facts about Lincoln by looking in a book. You can find the facts about the weather by looking out the window. In either case, the truth of the statement can be **verified** easily.

An opinion expresses an attitude or a feeling. Here are two examples.

Lincoln was the best president the United States ever had.
We have had too much rain this season.

Each of these opinions are **arguable**, that is, someone can read them and say, "I cannot agree with either of these statements. Give me your reasons." Because they can be argued, each one of them could be the thesis statement of a persuasive essay. A statement that doesn't have two sides can't, of course, be argued and isn't a good subject for a persuasive essay. The following would not be good subjects.

Lots of rainy weather makes me gloomy.
Pink is my favorite color.

---

### Practice 1

Decide which are facts and which are opinions. Write **F** beside each fact and **O** beside each opinion.

1. _____ A tiger is a striped, meat-eating animal that is a member of the cat family.

2. _____ The most strikeouts recorded by a pitcher in a major league game is 20.

3. _____ By far the greatest movie ever filmed is *Gone with the Wind*.

4. _____ Chocolate and tomatoes were foods used by the Aztecs of Mexico.

5. _____ Students should learn to type before they enter high school.

6. _____ Doing volunteer work in a hospital is a good way to find out if you would like a career in medicine.

7. _____ The President announced that the next space shuttle would go to Mars.

8. _____ Getting stains out of family clothes is an important job for a homemaker.

9. _____ Wearing the right clothes can make anyone popular.

10. _____ The dictionary tells you how to pronounce words.

When you try to change someone's mind, you need to give good reasons based on fact. You also want to be sure that you present things in a logical manner. If your reasons don't make sense, your reader will assume that you don't know what you are talking about. Here are some things to avoid when you are presenting your reasons.

## EITHER/OR THINKING

When you make your reader choose between two extremes, you are guilty of "either/or thinking." Here's an example.

> The superintendent says that students must get at least a C average if they want to play on school sports teams. If that rules goes through, we might as well stop playing right now.

This writer says that there are only two choices: Let everyone play on a team no matter what their average, or stop school sports. All the arguments in between—Is a C average too low or too high? Are the present student-players always poor students?—have not been mentioned. By leaving out the middle ground, the choice is limited and the argument is weak.

## RED HERRINGS

Some writers try to distract their readers from the issue by tossing in another idea. This technique is called a **red herring** from the old practice of drawing a dead fish across the trail to make pursuing dogs follow the wrong path. Here's an example.

> The superintendent says that students must get at least a C average if they want to play on school teams. This is another example of how wrong-headed our superintendent is. Doesn't she know that this is a democracy?

The writer has shifted the focus of the argument away from the original idea and introduced a new idea challenging the superintendent's patriotism.

## BANDWAGON PERSUASION

"To get on the bandwagon" means to do what everyone else is doing. Writers who use this technique want you to think that something is good just because everyone else is doing it. This kind of faulty thinking is frequently found in advertisements and in family discussions.

> I can get a ride to Marktree Beach for the class trip. We'll be gone for the whole weekend. Everyone is going. Is it OK?

There may be good reasons for going on the class trip. The fact that everyone else is going is not one of them.

## Practice 2

Read each statement. Decide which kind of faulty thinking it represents—***Either/Or Thinking***, ***Red Herring***, or ***Bandwagon***. Write your answer on the line below the statement. Underline the sentence that shows where the faulty thinking begins.

1. Lowden's Toothpaste has been recognized by the Dental Association as the toothpaste that contains all the right ingredients. It also makes your teeth white. After all, if your teeth aren't white, how can they be healthy?

   _____

2. Mayor Randolph Jarell has been accused by his opponents of awarding government contracts to his friends. This is an outright lie. After all, doesn't our mayor attend church every week with his family? He has a reading hour at the library every Thursday, and on Friday he teaches a class in civics at the high school.

   _____

3. This letter has been sent to you so that you can avoid an embarassing situation. Do you want to be the last person in your neighborhood to get an all-in-one black-and-white-and-color radio/TV? Everyone else on your block has one. Don't delay. Send this card in today.

   _____

4. Sarah's favorite sport is fishing. I don't think she'd like a trip to London.

   _____

5. My worthy opponent has said that I am against providing government money to educate good students who happen to be poor. My answer to that is simple. America has always been a land of opportunity. Abraham Lincoln and U.S. Grant came from poor families.

   _____

# Writing a Persuasive Essay

*A persuasive essay focuses on the audience, rather than on the subject or the writer.*

You can use the same facts in writing a persuasive essay, a personal essay, or an expository essay. You can even organize the essay in the same way. However, when your essay is finished, you want to be sure of two things:

- that your audience agrees with you
- that your audience is ready to act if action is called for

Gerry was given the following topic for a persuasive essay:

On the whole, technology does/does not make life better.

He had written two papers that described changes in technology—the kind of change usually called *progress*. His personal essay described the world he would know as an adult; his expository essay showed the world today. Gerry had to make a decision. How did he really feel about the changes that had already taken place in modern life?

He decided to make a list of pros and cons—things he thought were good and things he thought were not so good.

| PROS | CONS |
|---|---|
| space exploration | harming the environment |
| better education | nuclear war |
| easier living | people lose jobs |
| medicine saves lives | to machines |

Even though his columns were almost the same length, he realized that he felt very strongly that progress was a good thing. Problems could be solved by going forward and thinking of new solutions, not by going back. He was glad he had listed the objections, though. It showed that there were two sides to the issue. He would mention these in his essay to show his readers that he had looked at both sides. Finally, he decided that he wanted his readers to take a stand on something, not just to agree with him. He would ask them to support a new course entitled "Technology for Today and Tomorrow," which would help students to understand and plan for change. To make sure that he reached the people he wanted to reach, he wrote his essay as a Letter to the Editor for the school paper.

Here is the persuasive essay Gerry wrote. His personal essay is on the facing page so that you can compare the two. The notes in the margins point out some of the differences between them.

## A Look at the Future

In the year 2000 technology will dominate our lives so that even everyday events are almost unrecognizable. For one thing, the mornings begin in a different way. There aren't any alarm clocks anymore. Instead, a special device wakes me up by shaking me out of bed and onto the floor. The closet door opens automatically, and the exercise equipment rolls out. At the same time, the Robot—Cook begins heating the food pellets for breakfast. I am almost ready to leave for work.

*Gerry's personal essay has a different purpose—to tell his readers how he feels about something.*

Getting to work is very easy. No one needs a car. Right outside the door is a moving walkway tha takes me to a solar—powered transporter. It travels through the tubes that connect all the buildings in this area and stops right at my office. I open the door and step into a soundproof room filled with computer terminals.

*The descriptions are filled with details. The language is not obviously emotional.*

I have the same job as everyone else I know. I feed information into a huge computer that runs the city. Nobody likes this work, but there are no other kinds of jobs anymore. Fortunately, though, we only have to work for four hours a day, and then we can do what we want.

Some nights we ride the monorail around the mall to look at the lifelike robots that demonstrate the sports equipment. On weekends we go to synthesizer concerts. There aren't any live musicians, but we see 3—D videos while we listen to the music. Sometimes, though, what I like best is just to go home and spend the evening reading. I don't turn on any machines. I just read from a real book, not a computer.

*Gerry uses the first person, instead of the "editorial we" throughout.*

It will be hard to get away from machines in the year 2000. Technology will make life easier, but it will also make life more artificial. People will never have to cook a meal, get wet when it rains, or drive in traffic jams. On the other hand, people will never have a chance to taste fresh strawberries, hear a live concert, or even drive their own cars. By taking care of everything for everybody, technology will take away our chance to enjoy life directly.

*In his concluding paragraph Gerry uses dramatic images ("tasting fresh strawberries") to show how stongly he feels. He has not asked us to change our minds about the future, just to understand how he feels. He succeeds.*

To the Editor:

We like to think of modern technology as something that makes life better. However, one look at the daily headlines shows us all the bad things that happen as a result of technology. We read about the pollution of the environment. We worry about nuclear war. Even in our daily lives, we know that the computer has taken away a lot of jobs. So what good does all this technological change do? Let's look around us.

It is morning at Mountainside Hospital. A young woman who has been blind from birth is having a special eye operation. Soon she will be able to see. Every day medical technology makes life better. Artificial hearts work, and so do artificial legs and hands. When we go to school, we use a computer to design things that used to take us hours to draw by hand. It also makes writing easier. Outside of school, a computer tells us when something is wrong with the car. It lets us know that we need oil or gas or a new battery.

Unfortunately, not all the problems of the world are solved by technology. There are still wars. There is still famine and poverty. People in poorer countries do not live as long as Americans. In our own country there are still too many poor people. There is also too much pollution. The world we live in is not a perfect place, but I'm not sure that it ever can be. I do know this, however, that stopping progress and technology won't make things better.

Our generation has a chance to make a difference. We can sit back and say that technology just doesn't work. Or we can learn all we can about our problems and start to think about ways to solve them. We don't have to wait until we're out of college, either. Next Tuesday the school board will ask us to vote on a new course called ''Technology for Today and Tomorrow.'' We can look at the world around us——and we can say yes.

**Your Essay** WP

On a separate sheet of paper, write a persuasive essay on the following topic:

> Pick a period of time you are familiar with and convince your reader that this was/ would be a good time in which to live. (You can't use the present.)

Use Gerry's persuasive essay as a model. Remember that your purpose is to persuade your audience to your point of view. You can write your essay as an editorial and use "we" if you wish.

Follow these steps to write your essay:

1. *Narrow the topic.* Choose a time period you are interested in and that you know something about. This is not a research paper. However, you will want to choose a period of time that you can state some facts about. You might want to write about the 50's or 60's, when your parents were teenagers. Or your knowledge of science fiction might make it easy for you to make up details about a future world. Whatever you choose, make sure you feel strongly about your choice.

2. *Brainstorm.* Use the prewriting stage to brainstorm details on both sides—what is good about the time period you chose and what is bad.

3. *Write a first draft.* Begin with a clear statement of what you have chosen to write about. You may follow Gerry's example and list some of the objections your audience might raise to your choice. For example, if you begin by saying "The 1960's was a time of change. It was exciting and filled with new ideas." You might add. "Of course, not everyone agreed with what was going on." Write a second paragraph that presents your choice in the best possible light. Use emotion when you can, but use good thinking too. In the third paragraph, try to answer your reader's objections. Then, in the final paragraph, pull out all the stops. Make your readers feel what you feel.

4. *Revise your essay.* Do you want to improve the opening or the closing? Have you used good thinking throughout? Do you need to add any details? Do you need to take out anything that does not belong? Do you need to add transitions? Are there any words that need changing? Do you want to combine ideas?

5. *Edit and proofread your essay.* Then make a clean copy.

# *How to Write Under Pressure*

*Short cuts help you write a timed essay.*

The process of writing is always the same, whether you are writing a book, a research paper, an essay, or the answer to a test question. When you are writing a timed essay, though, you need to condense some of the steps. You cannot spend much time on prewriting, and you cannot count on having time to revise, edit, and copy what you write. However, you will be able to use some easy tricks that have worked for many other writers faced with the need to write quickly and well.

1. Know ahead of time how many minutes you are going to spend on each part of the writing process.
2. Go into the test planning to write about something you know very well.
3. Make a short list or a diagram to show the main points you plan to cover.
4. Choose your transition words before you begin writing.
5. Begin the essay by restating the topic.
6. As you write, be aware of places where you might want to combine, take out, or change things.
7. Make a final check of your essay.

**1. *Know ahead of time how many minutes you are going to spend on each part of the writing process.***

Because your time is limited, you need to plan carefully how to use it. Most of the time should be spent on actually writing the essay, with a few minutes for prewriting at the beginning and a few for revising and editing at the end. If you finish prewriting in less than the time you have allowed, use the extra minutes for revising and editing. Here are some suggested ways to divide your time.

FOR A 30-MINUTE ESSAY
Spend 5 minutes on prewriting.
Spend 20 minutes on writing.
Spend 5 minutes on revising and editing.

FOR A 45-MINUTE ESSAY
Spend 7 or 8 minutes on prewriting.
Spend 30 minutes on writing.
Spend 7 or 8 minutes on revising and editing.

FOR A 60-MINUTE ESSAY
Spend 7 or 8 minutes on prewriting.
Spend 45 minutes on writing.
Spend 7 or 8 minutes on revising and editing.

**Practice 1**

Show how much time you would spend on each part of the writing process under the following circumstances.

a. For a 60-minute essay

_____ prewriting

_____ writing

_____ revising and editing

b. For a 45-minute essay

_____ prewriting

_____ writing

_____ revising and editing

c. For a 30-minute essay

_____ prewriting

_____ writing

_____ revising and editing

## 2. Go into the test planning to write about something you know very well.

The assigned topic for a timed essay is often very general. The test writers make it this way so that everyone will have a fair chance. You can turn this to your advantage by deciding ahead of time what focus you will use for the topic. If you like sports, plan to give the topic—whatever it is—a sports focus. If music is what you know best, decide in advance that you will use a music theme in your essay.

T. J. is a good pitcher and a baseball fan. This is the topic he was given:

*If you could relive some part of your life, what incident would you choose and why?*

T. J. had already decided that whatever the topic was, he would choose a sports focus. He now had only one decision to make—would he write about a baseball game he saw or a baseball game he played in? He made two columns on his paper and wrote the following:

| *WHAT* | *WHY* |
|---|---|
| *pitching a no-hitter last year* | *proud and excited* |

T. J. was off to a good start. He knew what he was going to write about, and he knew how he felt about the subject.

**Practice 2**

What do you know a lot about? What do you really care about? Choose something that means a lot to you. Decide that this will be the focus of your essay—no matter what. Read the topic and fill in the blanks in the What/Why columns.

*If you could relive some part of your life, what incident would you choose and why?*

<u>WHAT</u>                                          <u>WHY</u>

_____                    _____

### 3. *Make a short list or diagram to show the points you plan to cover.*

Once you have decided on the focus of your essay, write down as many details as you can as quickly as you can. If you can arrange them in some kind of order, do so—but don't spend time worrying about it.

T.J.'s list of details looked like this.

<u>*WHAT*</u>

*pitching a no-hitter*
*last inning—faced toughest hitters*
*great catch saved me—2nd inning*
*3rd inning—too many walks*
*got nervous in 5th inning*
*two on base in the 9th*
*crowd got quiet in 7th*

<u>*WHY*</u>

*proud and excited*
*meant state championship*
*personal best*

Here is another way to list details. Instead of writing **What** and **Why**, T.J. made two large circles. Then he put all the details on lines that came from the circles.

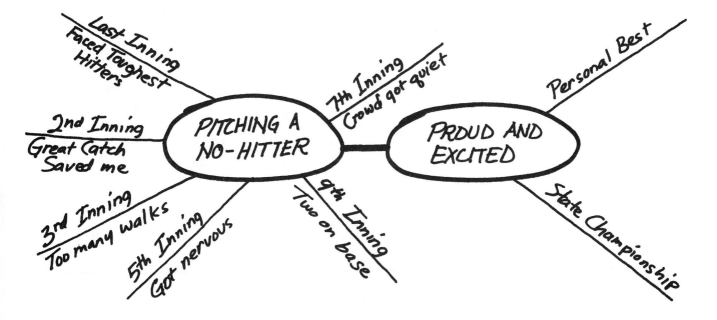

121

## Practice 3

First, write a list and then make a diagram of details for the focus you chose in Practice 2. Try both techniques and see which one you prefer.

DETAILS

WHAT                                          WHY

_____

_____

_____

_____

_____

_____

_____

_____

_____

_____

_____

DIAGRAM

## 4. Choose your transition words before you begin writing.

Before you begin writing, choose the order you want to arrange the details in. Since many assigned topics begin by asking the writer to describe or tell about something, using time order for these details makes the writing task easier. When you are given a topic, decide whether you can use time order in all or part of your essay. If you are listing details, the ones under WHAT are the details to look at.

T.J. looked at the list of details he had written under WHAT. They could easily be arranged in time order. He divided them into three groups—the beginning, the middle, and the end—and numbered the details 1, 2, or 3.

*WHAT*
*pitching a no-hitter*
*last inning—faced toughest hitters* **3**
*great catch saved me—2nd inning* **1**
*3rd inning—too many walks* **1**
*got nervous in 5th inning* **2**
*two on base in the ninth* **3**
*crowd got quiet in 7th* **2**

*WHY*
*proud and excited*
*meant state championship*
*personal best*

Then he chose these transitions, wrote them at the bottom of the list, and numbered them.

*at the beginning of the game* **1**
*halfway through the game* **2**
*finally* **3**

T. J. had made a working outline in no time at all! All the details numbered 1 would follow transition 1; all the details numbered 2 would follow transition 2; all the details numbered 3 would follow transition 3.

What about the details he had written under the WHY heading? When T. J. looked at them, he realized that they were just what he needed for his opening and closing.

---

### Practice 4

Go back to Practice 3 and look at the details you put under WHAT. Arrange them in time order by giving them numbers. Use 1 and 2 if your story falls naturally in two parts. Use 1, 2, 3 or 1, 2, 3, 4 if it follows some other sequence. Choose transition words that tie the parts together and number them as well.

TRANSITION WORDS

_____

_____

_____

_____

_____

### 5. *Begin the essay by restating the topic.*

A simple way to write the opening sentence of an essay is to restate the topic. For the topic "If you could relive some part of your life, what incident would you choose and why?" Kirsten decided to write about the time she and her older sister went on a backpacking trip. All she needed to do was change the question into a statement. Then she filled in the incident she had chosen and her reasons. Here is the opening sentence Kirsten wrote:

> If I could relive some part of my life, I would choose the two weeks my sister and I spent backpacking in the Smoky Mountains because it was an experience that made me feel as though I could handle anything.

**Practice 5**

You have been given the following topic:

> If you could go back in time and do things differently, what incident would you choose to relive and why?

You are going to write about the time you and your father had a fight and did not talk to each other for two days. You would like to relive that incident because you said things that were unfair and hurt his feelings.

Use this information to turn the topic into an opening sentence.

_____

_____

_____

_____

### 6. *As you write, be aware of places where you might want to combine, take out, or change things.*

Even though you will not have much time for revision as a separate step, you can revise your essay as you write. Use a combination of these techniques:

a. Think ahead as you write. Think of your notes, diagram, or list of points to cover as a kind of first draft. As you turn them into the paragraphs and sentences of your essay, decide whether you want to change the order, add details, or take anything out. You can indicate these changes in your prewriting notes or just make them as you write the essay.

b. Plan to write only one draft of your essay. If you need to revise, make changes right on that draft. Remember that it is better to turn in an essay with handwritten changes on it than to make no changes at all. Leave enough space in the margins and between lines to insert changes.

Here are some of Richard's prewriting notes and part of his essay for the topic "Tell about something important that you did not learn in school." Notice both the changes he made as he wrote and the changes he inserted afterwards.

## Richard's prewriting notes

Learned to trust my own judgment

school—did what other people told me to
—never had a chance to make decisions

camp —forced to take charge
—scared at first

home —parents made the rules
—criticized my decisions

## Richard's essay

. . . I had never learned to trust my own judgment before. Both at school and at home, other people made the rules. I just did what they ~~made me do.~~ *told me to.* At school, students were never given a chance to make decisions. In fact, we could be punished for deciding things on our own. At home, the few times that I tried to take charge, my parents discouraged me*, disagreeing with my decisions and even criticizing them.* ~~They never agreed with my decisions. They even criticized them.~~

The first time I was left alone with a group of campers, I was terrified. I had no choice, though. . . .

## Practice 6

Use your prewriting notes from Practice 3 to write a sample paragraph. As you turn your notes into sentences, do at least two of the following things:

- Add a detail
- Take out a detail
- Change the position of a detail
- Combine two or more ideas
- Change a word or group of words

You can make your changes as part of the process of writing the paragraph, or you can insert changes after you have finished writing.

_____

_____

_____

_____

_____

_____

_____

_____

_____

_____

_____

_____

## 7. Make a final check of the following points.

1. Have you covered the assigned topic?
2. Have you included enough details to support your ideas?
3. Have you put your ideas in an order that makes sense?
4. Have you used complete sentences?
5. Have you used words correctly?
6. Have you followed the rules for capitalization, spelling, and punctuation?
7. Have you written neatly and made your revisions clearly enough to be read?